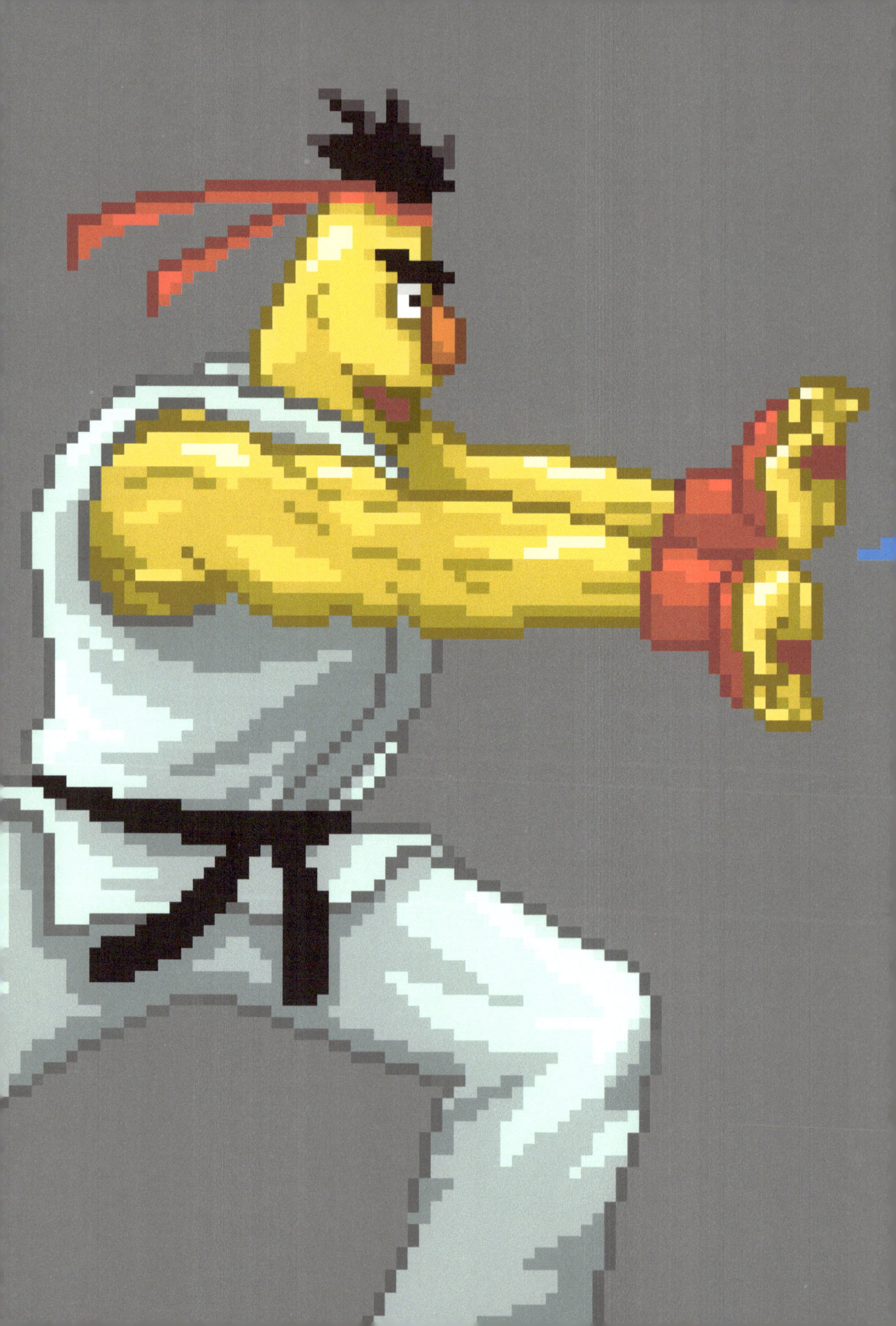

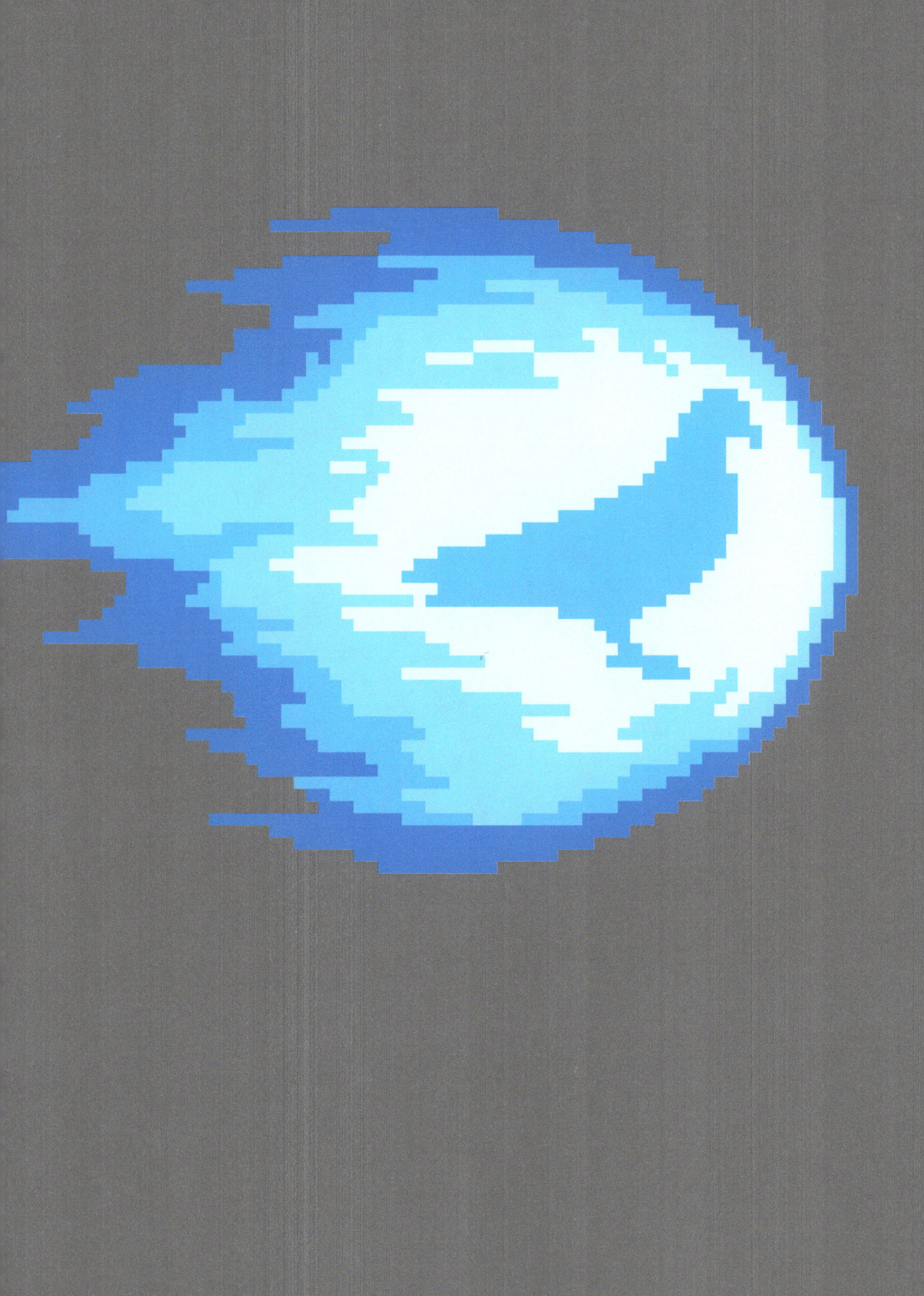

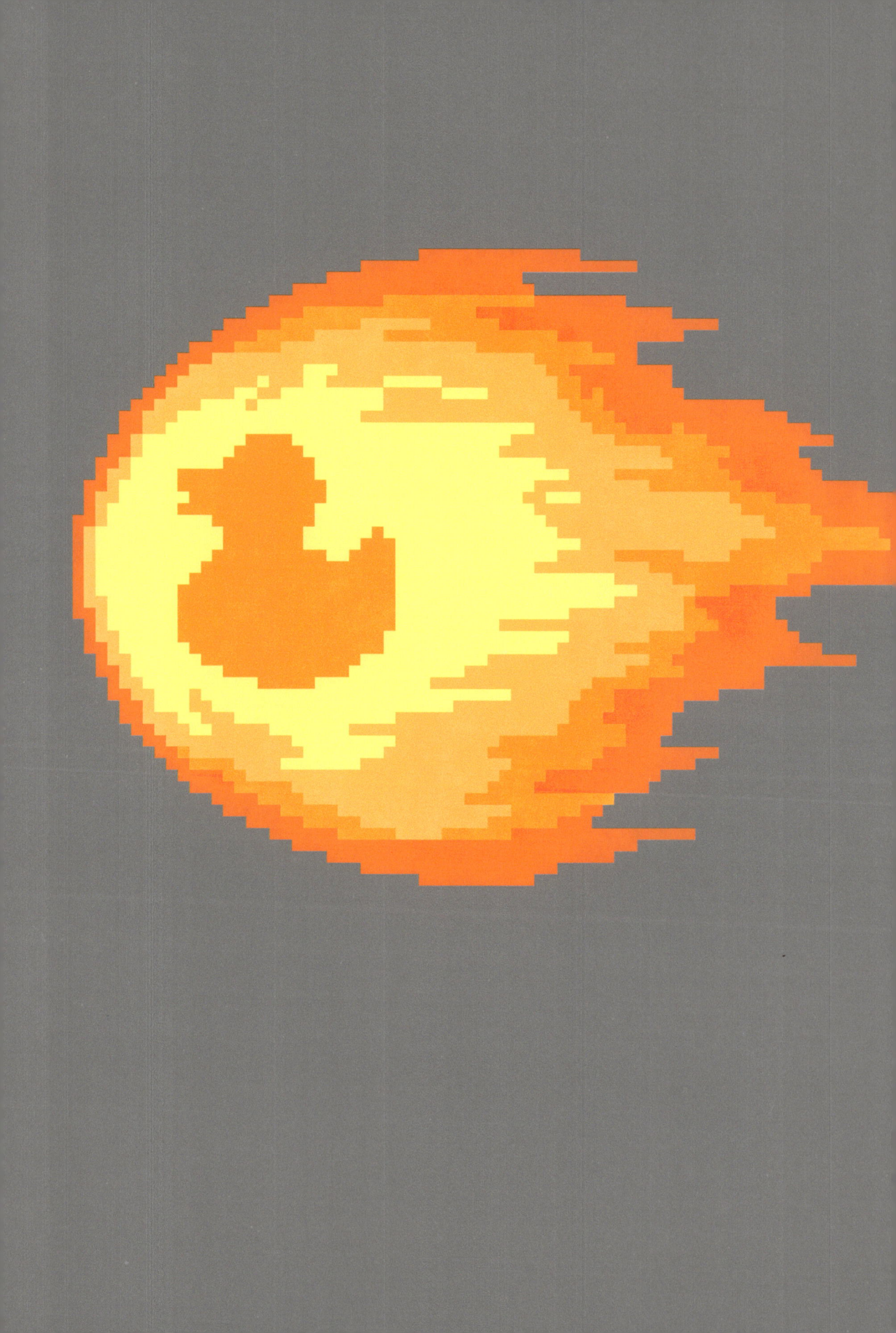

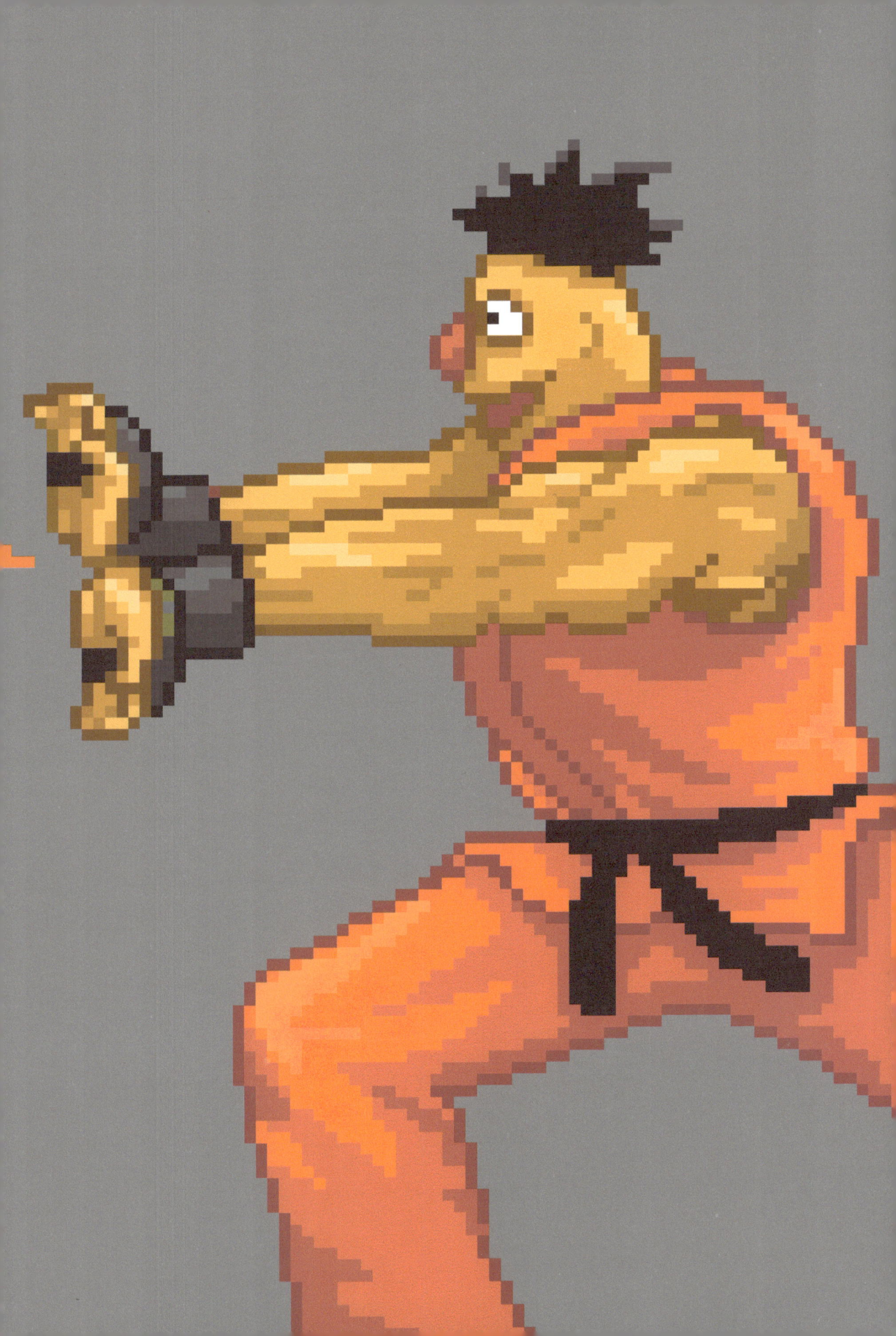

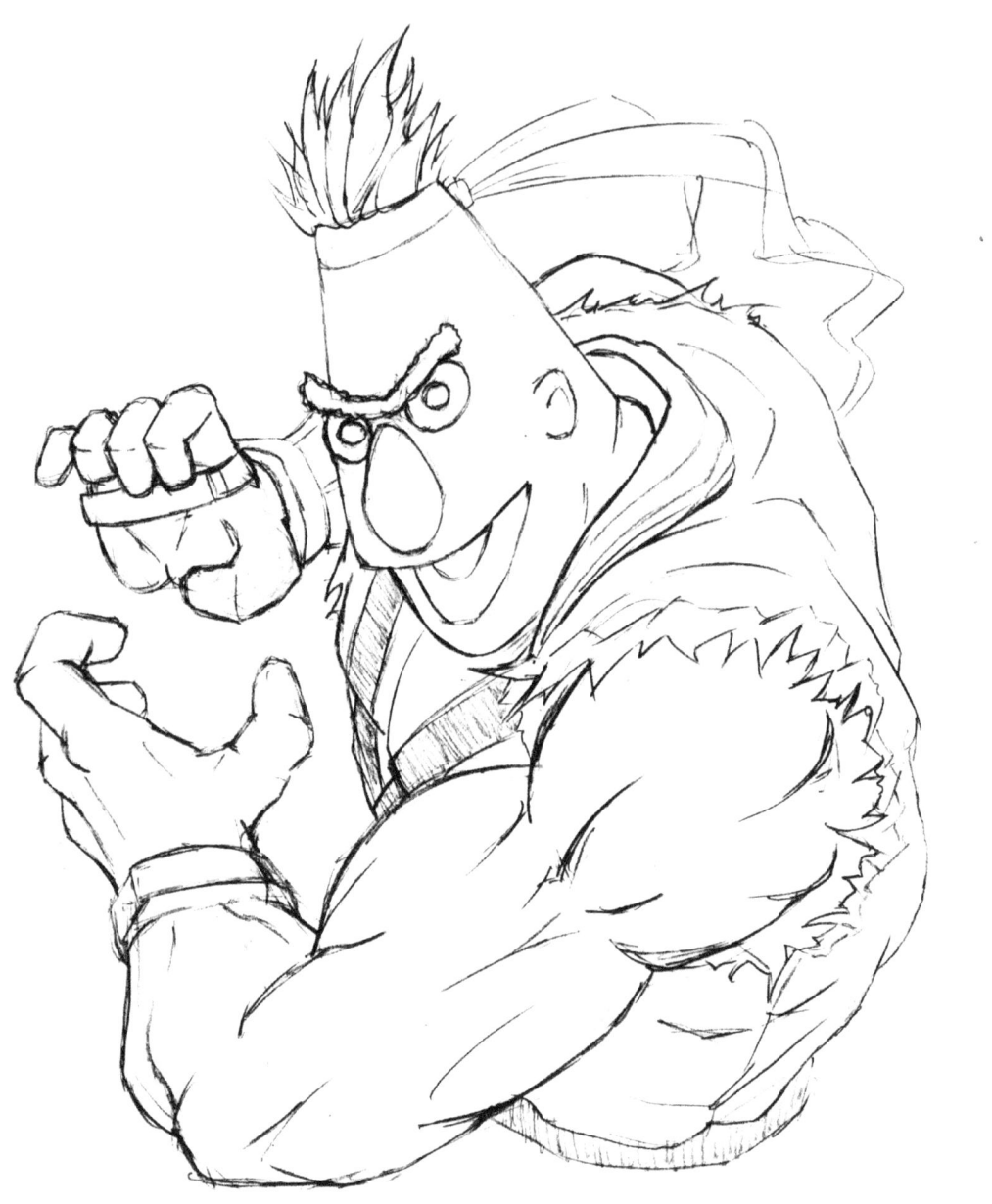

Super Sesame Street Fighter Art Book
© 2014

ISBN-13: 978-1495949623

ISBN-10: 1495949621

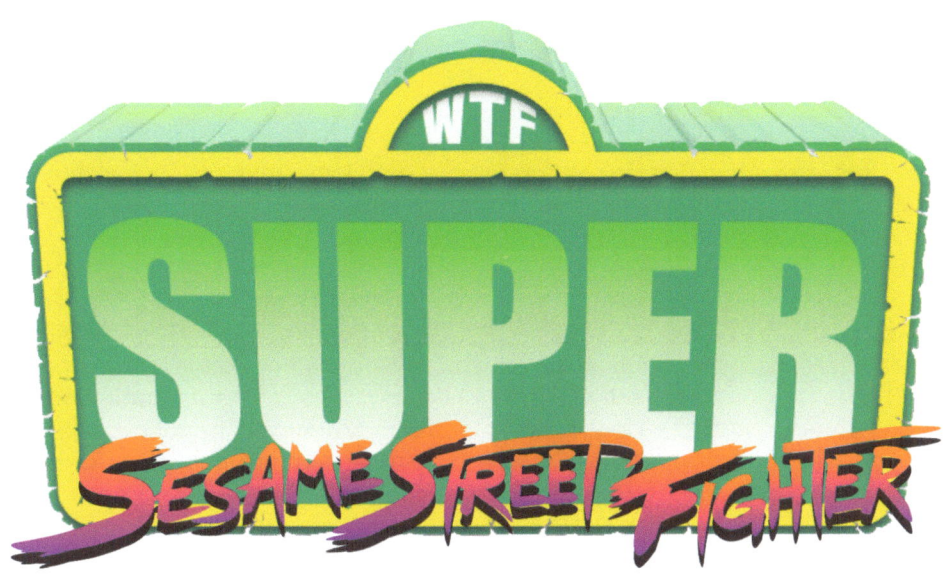

ART BOOK

Matt Crane

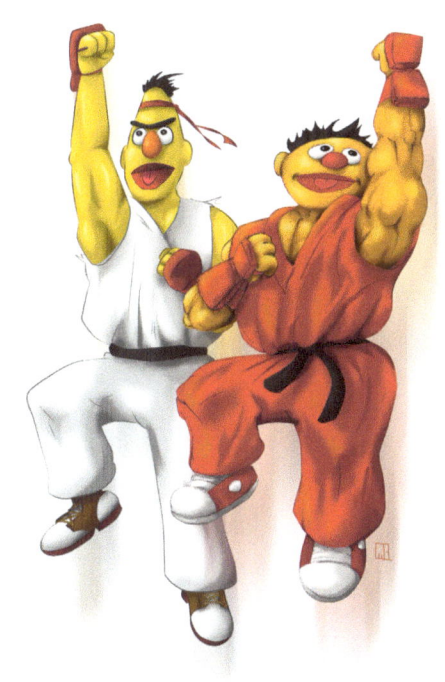

When I was a kid I loved *Sesame Street*. When I became a

teen, I fell in love with *Street Fighter II*. Somewhere in my muddled teenage mind I got the idea to combine the two, and for reasons I don't fully understand, that idea has stuck with me throughout the years.

As I grew up, graduated from college, and started my career as a graphic designer the idea continued to haunt me. When I heard that Capcom was bringing its premiere fighting game franchise out of a long period of dormancy with *Street Fighter IV*, it gave me some added motivation to stop dreaming and finally start doing a Sesame Street Fighter illustration series.

For a while I hesitated to create these illustrations because I didn't think it would be respectful to Jim Henson, for whom I have a ton of admiration. However, after watching some of the older *Muppet Show* episodes and enjoying the slightly more edgy and violent humor, I came to the conclusion that Jim might actually get a good laugh out of the idea. I don't want to be presumptuous and put words into a dead genius' mouth, but if you look at how much parody humor came out of *Sesame Street* and the *Muppet Show*, I think it's reasonable to suppose that Jim would understand that these illustrations are created out of love for his characters and not meant to be hurtful or disparaging.

So, on March 16, 2009 I posted my first "finished" illustration of Kernie (Ken + Ernie) on *DeviantArt.com*. I got enough positive feedback that I decided to keep going with it, and have been enjoying the process of adding new characters to the series ever since.

I'm certainly not the first or the *only* artist to come up with this concept, but I feel safe in saying that I've been the most prolific. I've been blessed to have my work featured on prominent web sites like *Game Pro* (a magazine I subscribed to as a teen in the 90s), *Kotaku*, and *Capcom-unity* (by none other than Seth Killian himself). Recently, I was also pleasantly surprised to find that a talented game developer created a Sesame Street Fighter typing video game that was inspired by my work! This game along with my artwork were featured on some mainstream web sites like *Wired* and *USA Today*, which was incredibly awesome.

The artwork in this book includes some of my earliest drawings from junior high and college as well as my more recent illustrations. I hope you enjoy them, and if you're an artist who enjoys this kind of parody work, I hope they inspire you to create your own special brand of weirdness.

Matt Crane (gavacho13)
March 2014

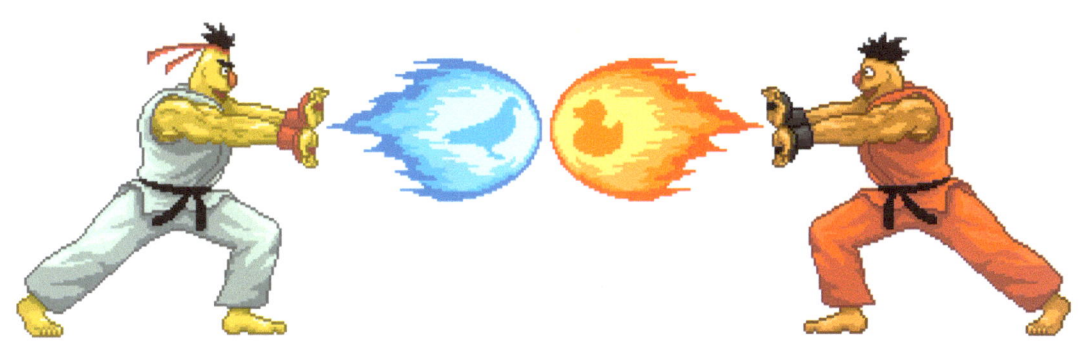

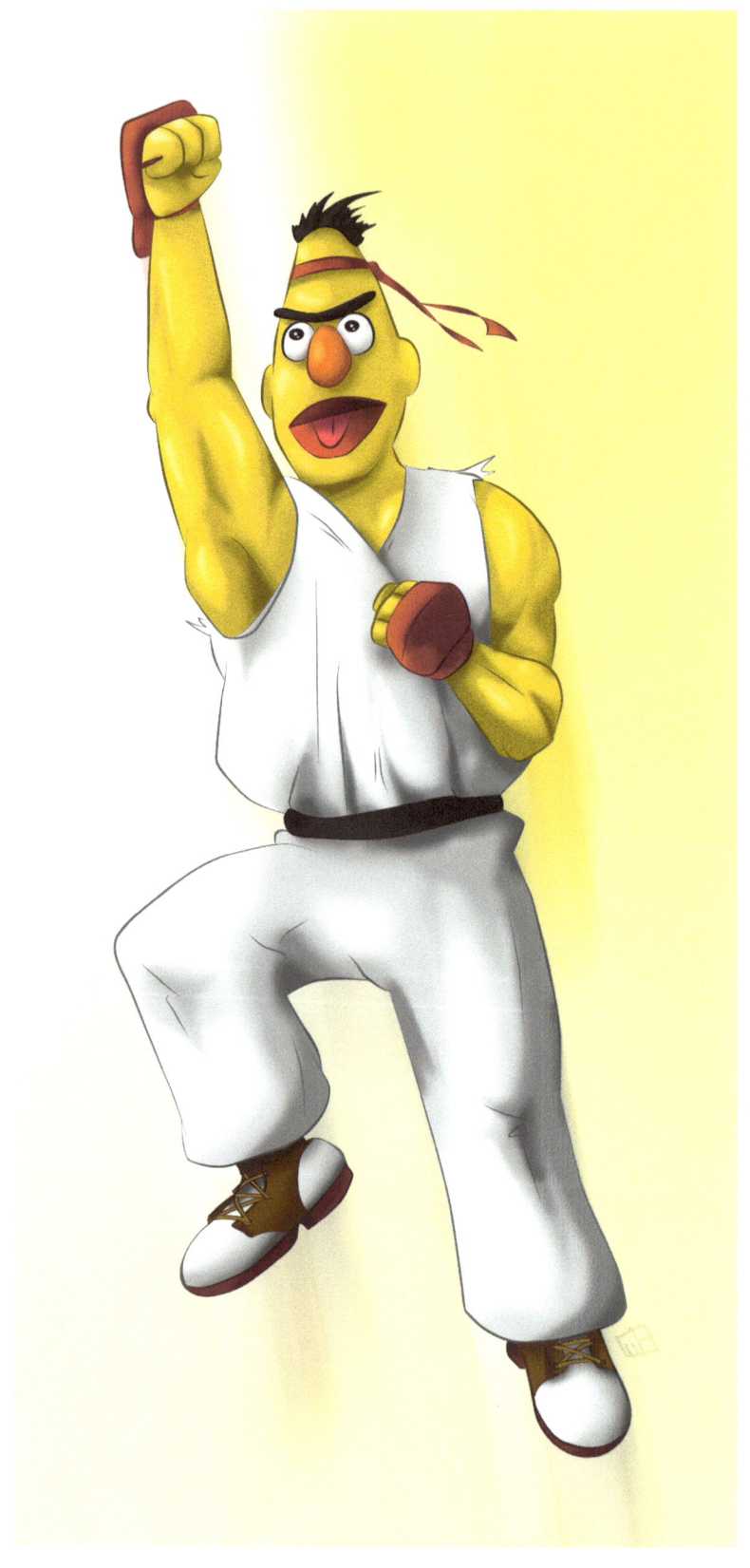

BERYU

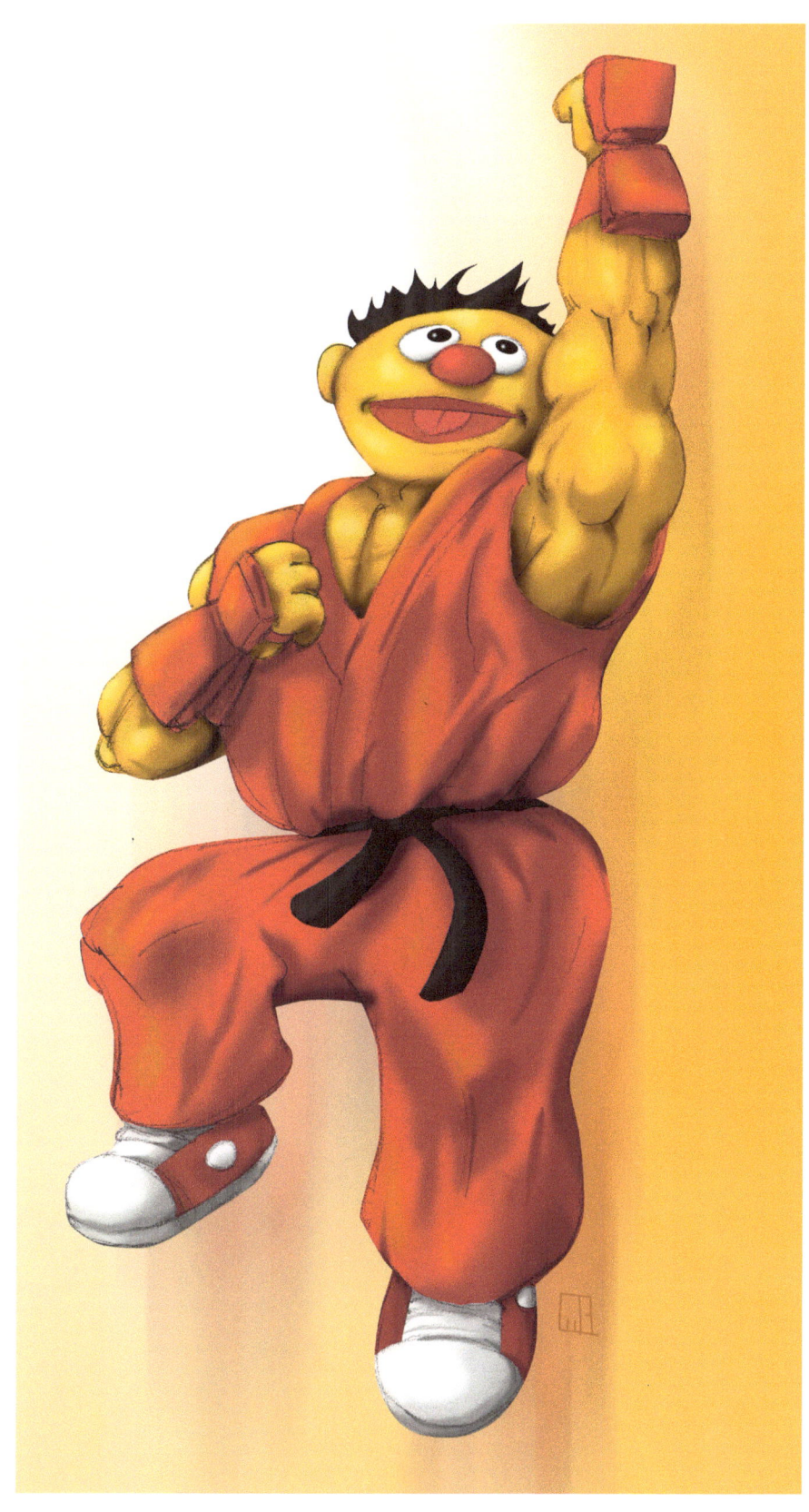

KERNIE

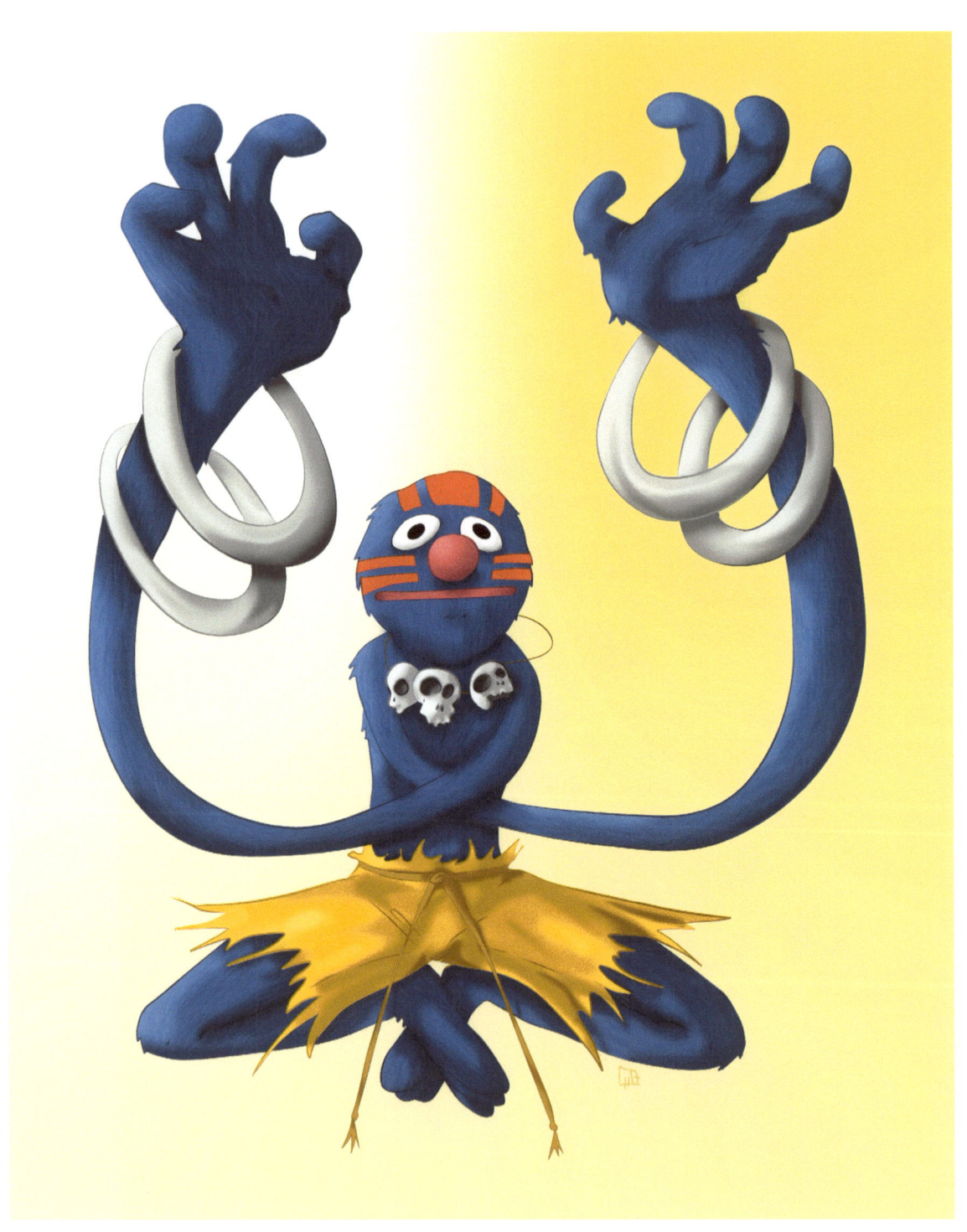

GRHALSIM

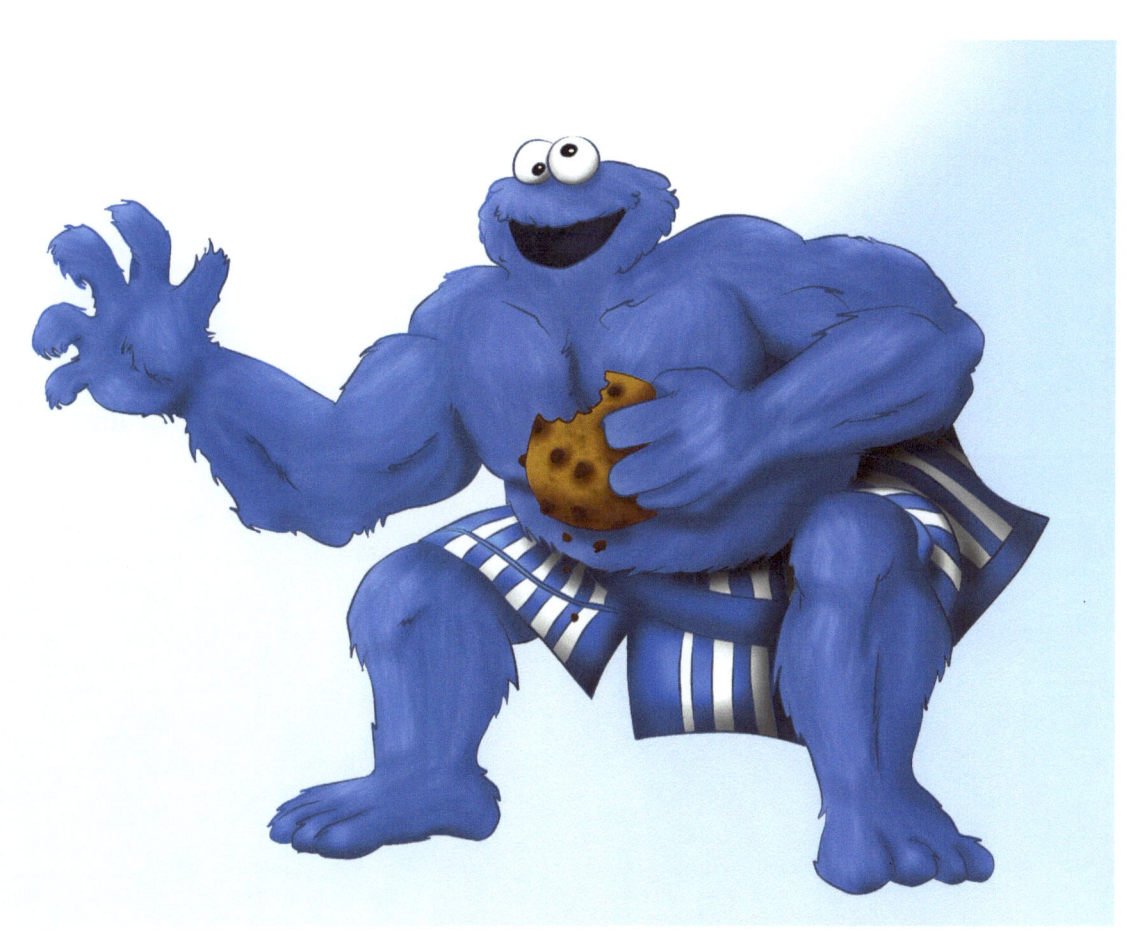

C. MONDA

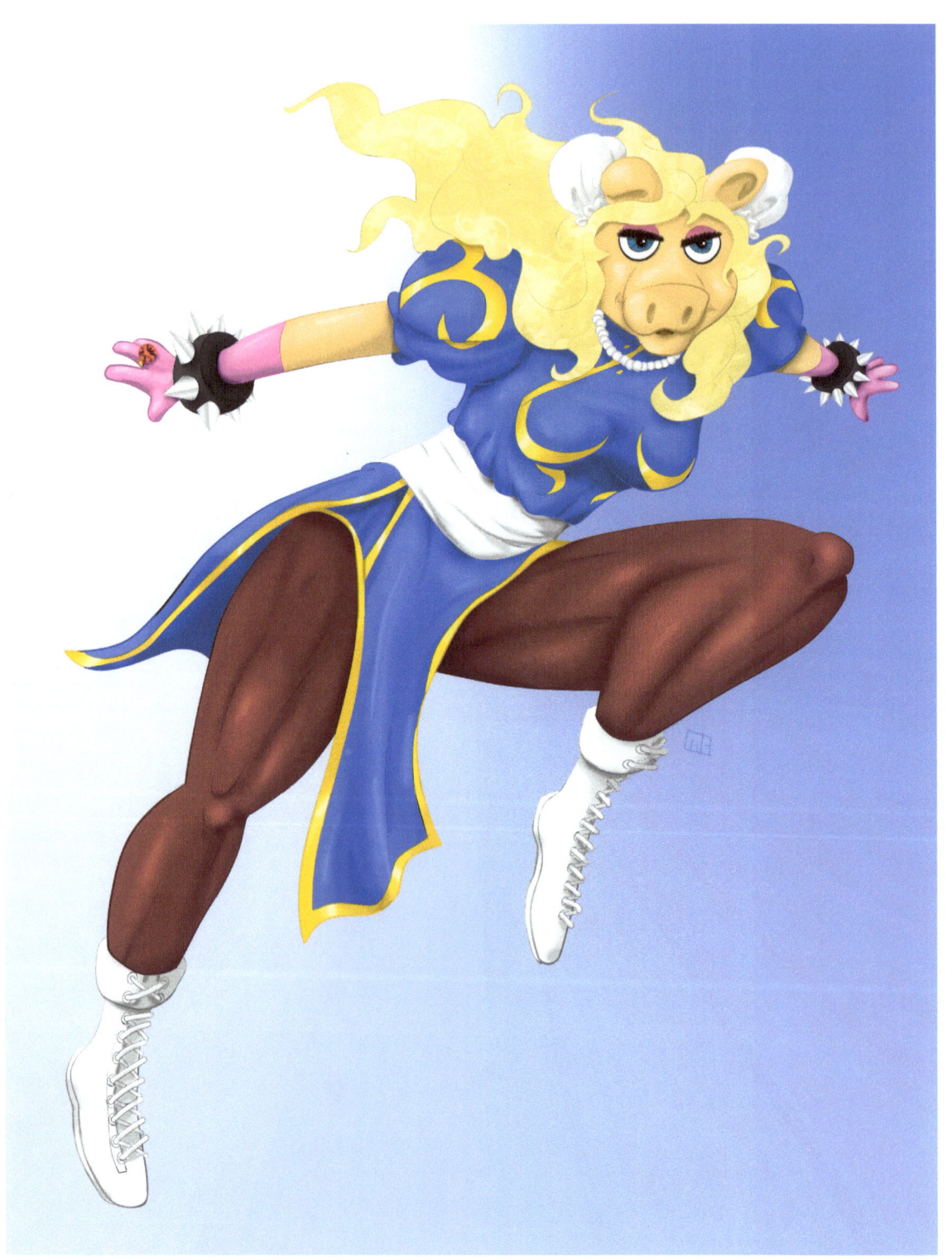

PIG-LI

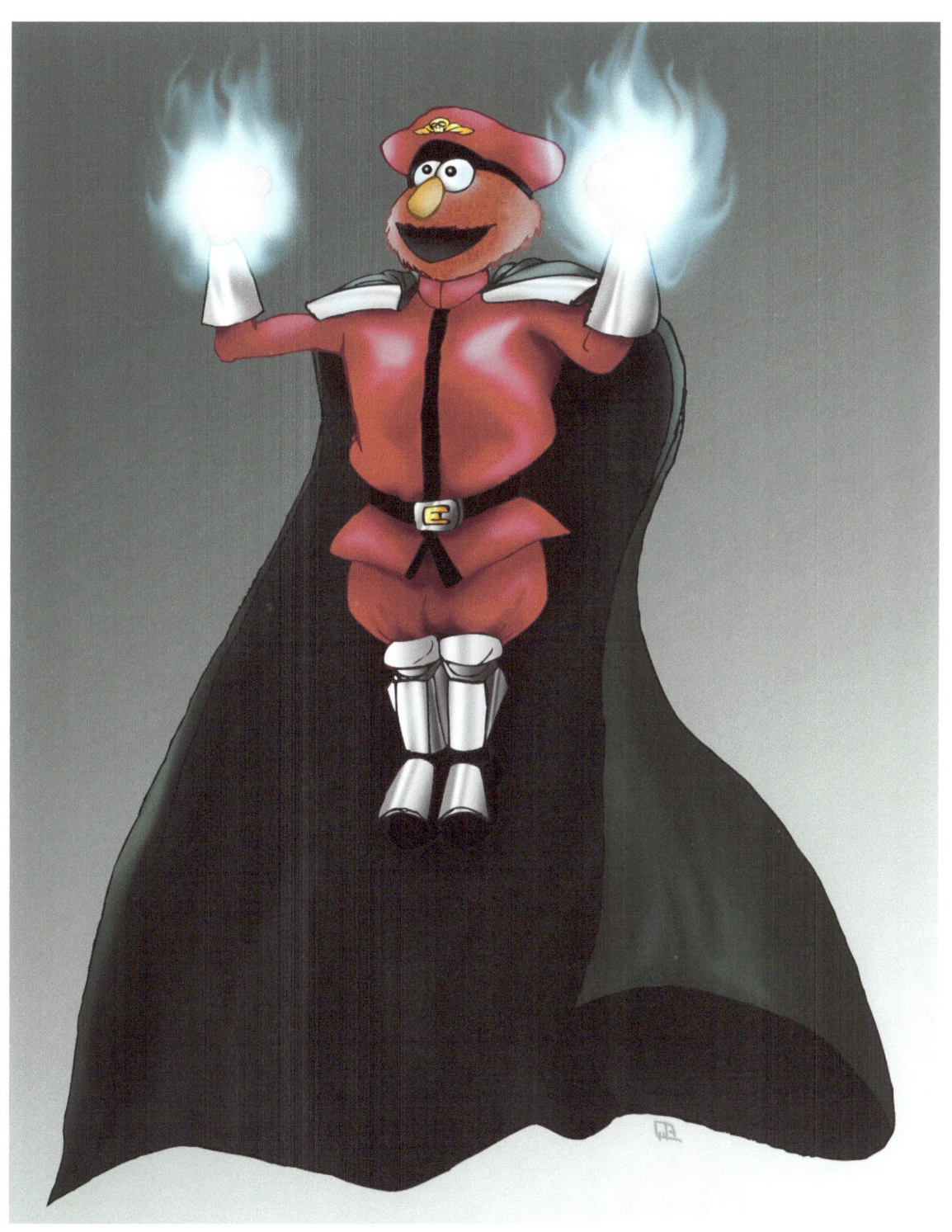

ELMO BISON

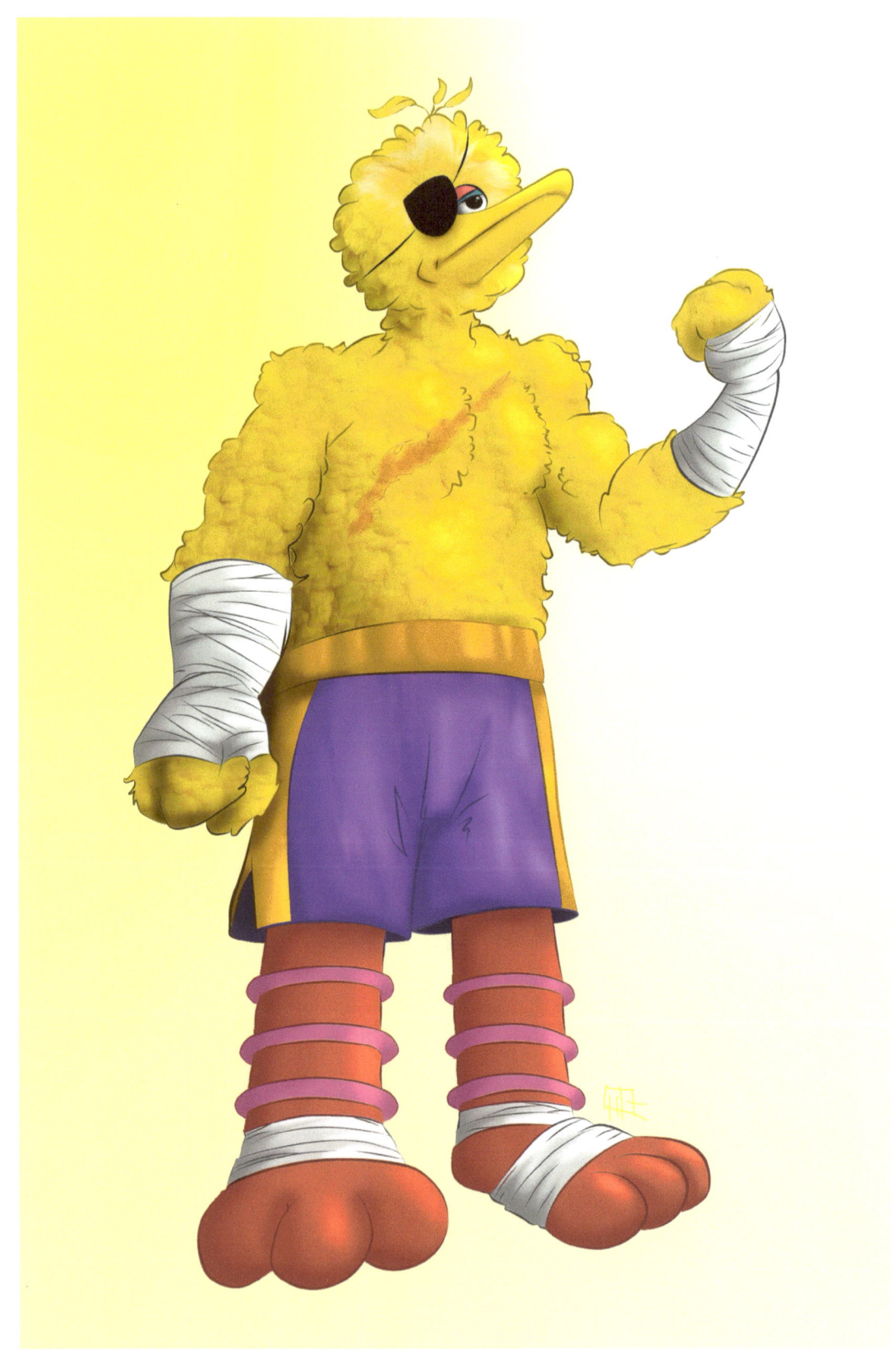

BIG BAGAT

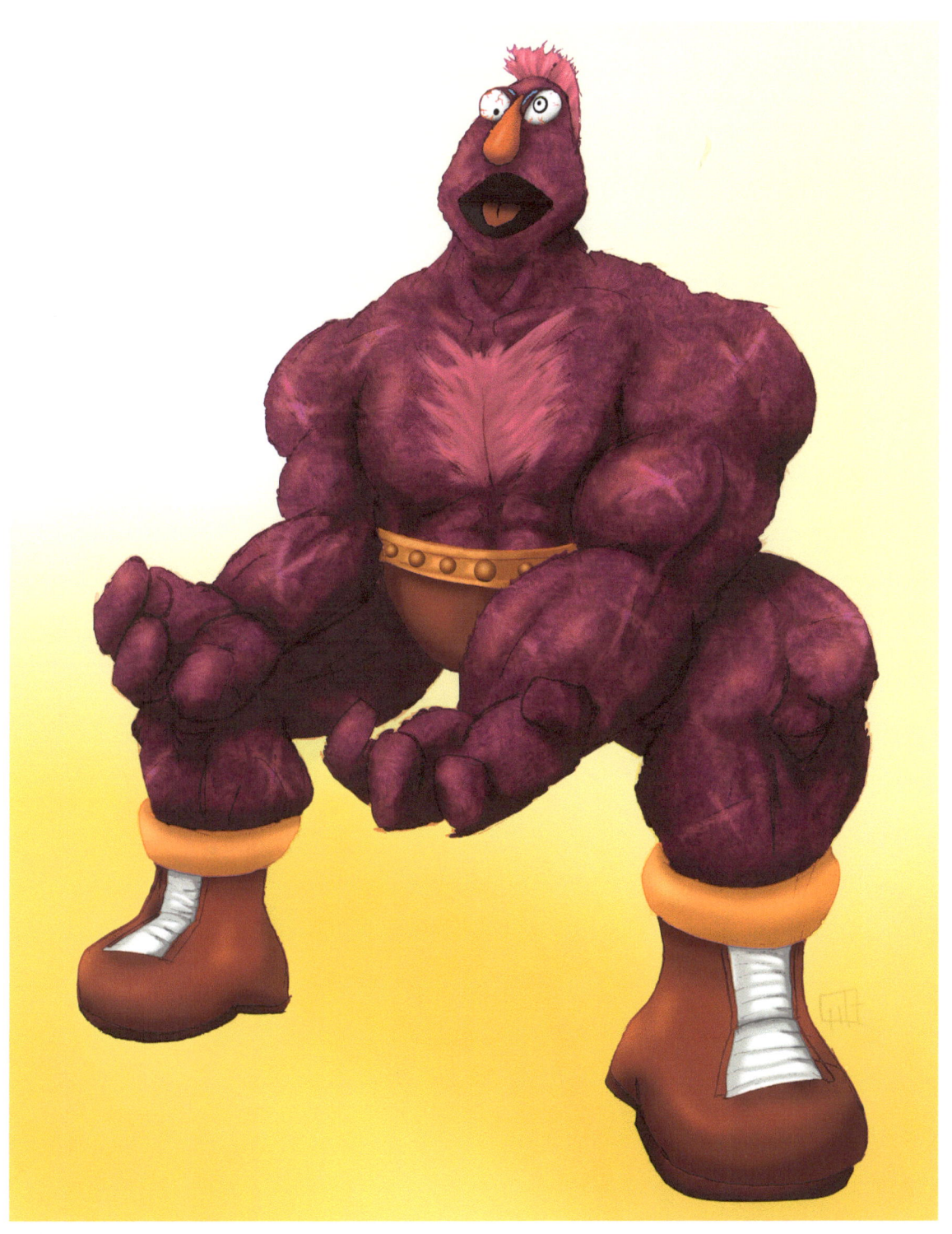

ZELLYGIEF

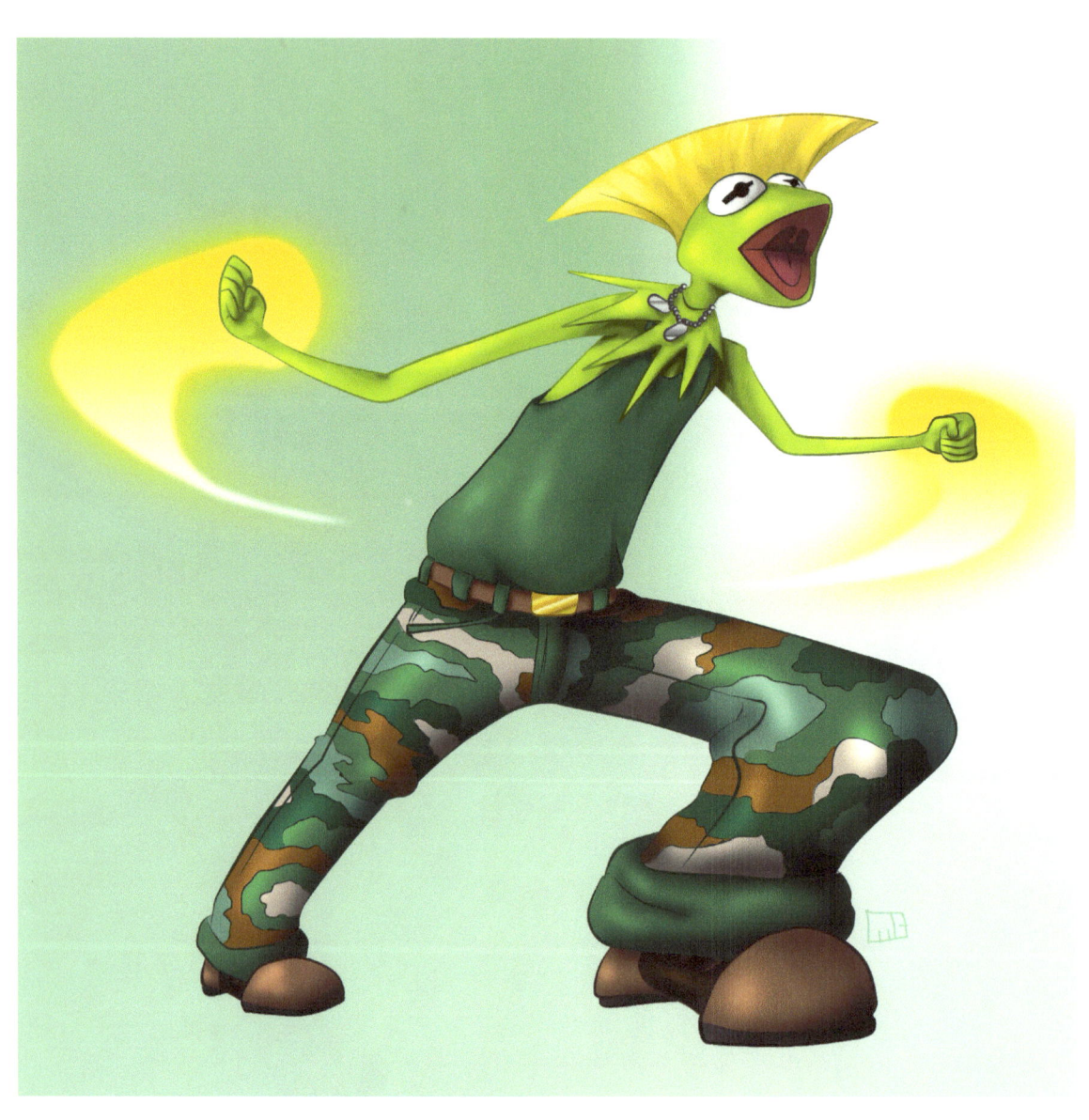

GURMIT

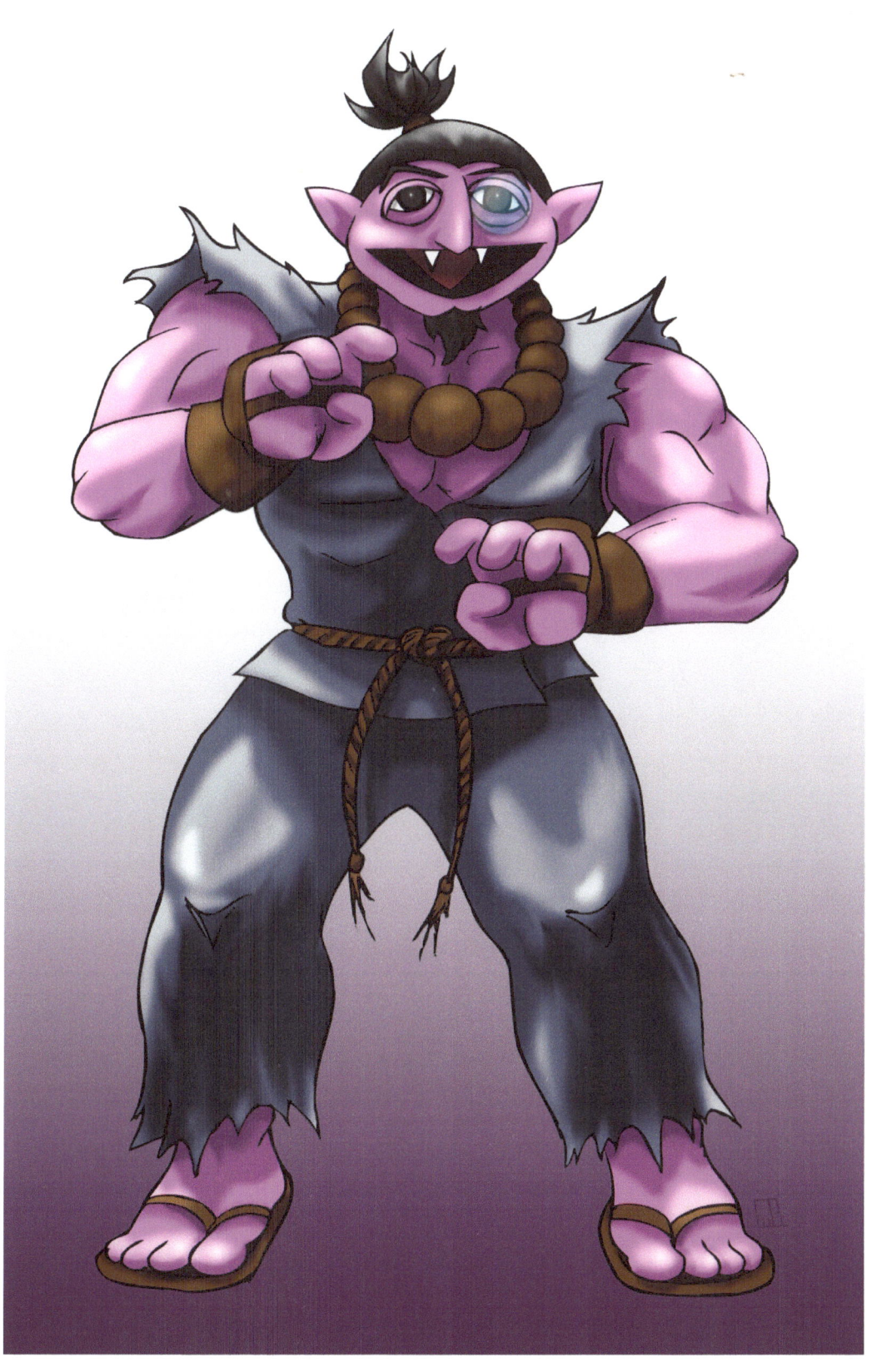

ACOUNTMA

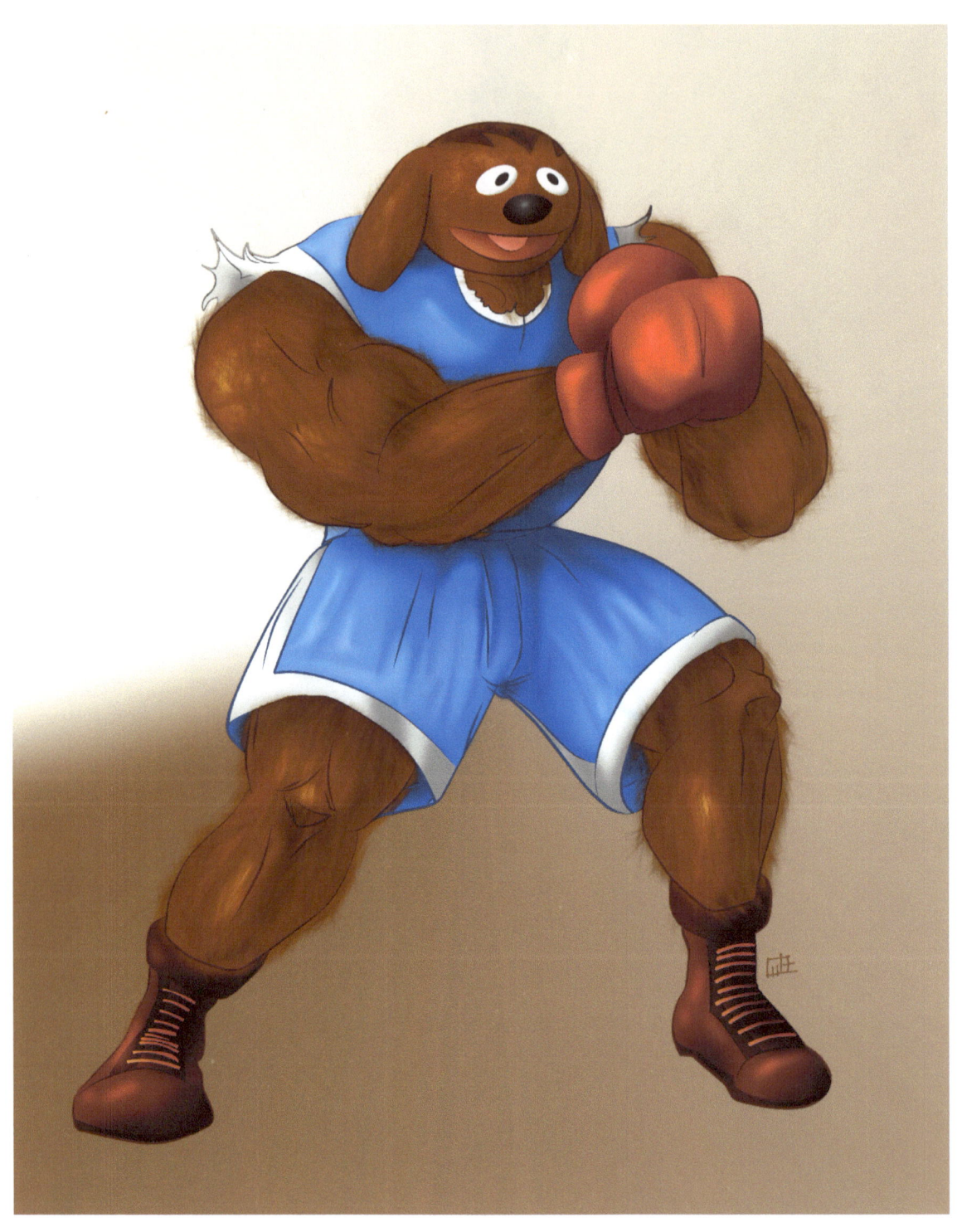

BALDOG

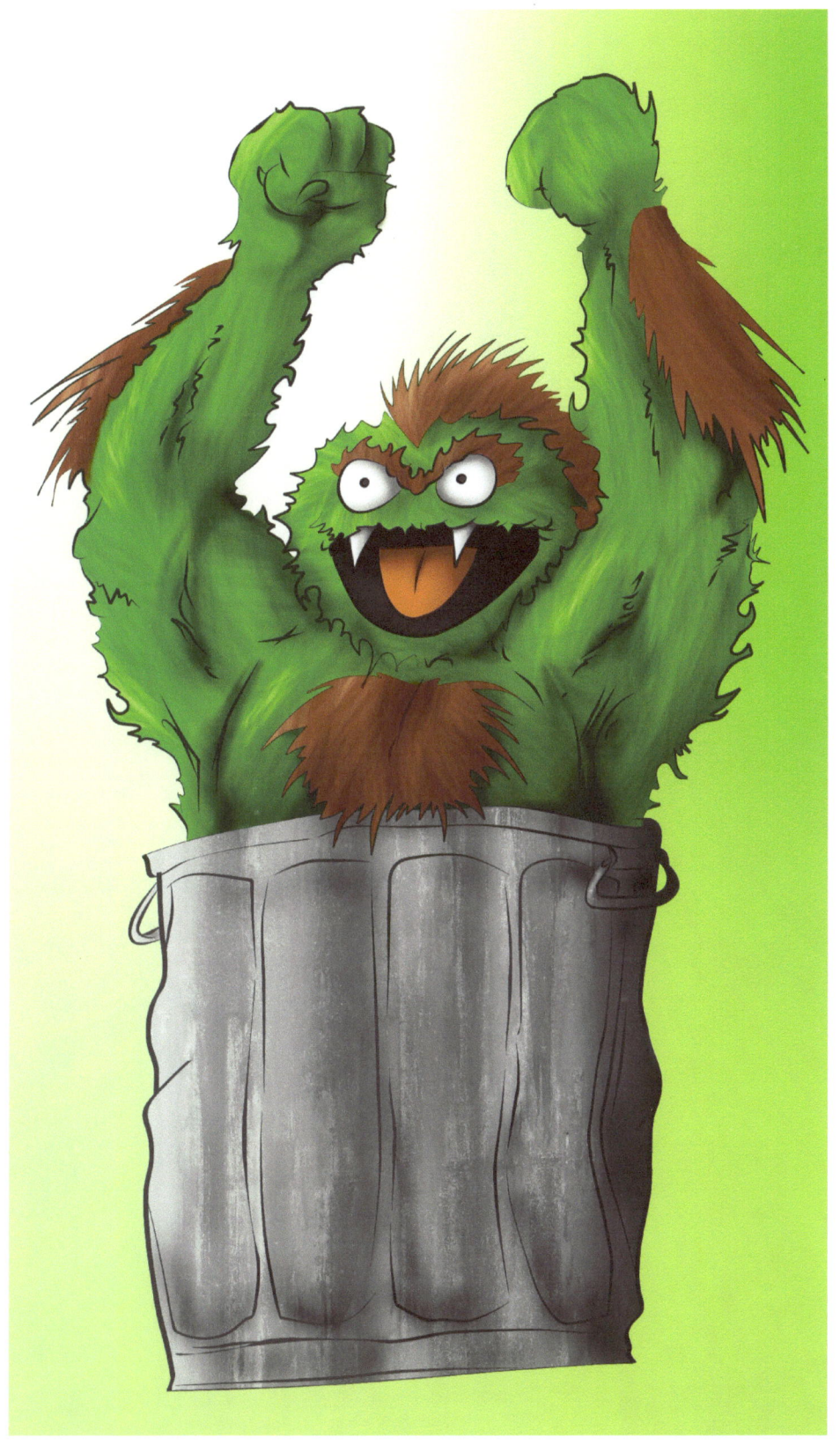

OSKA

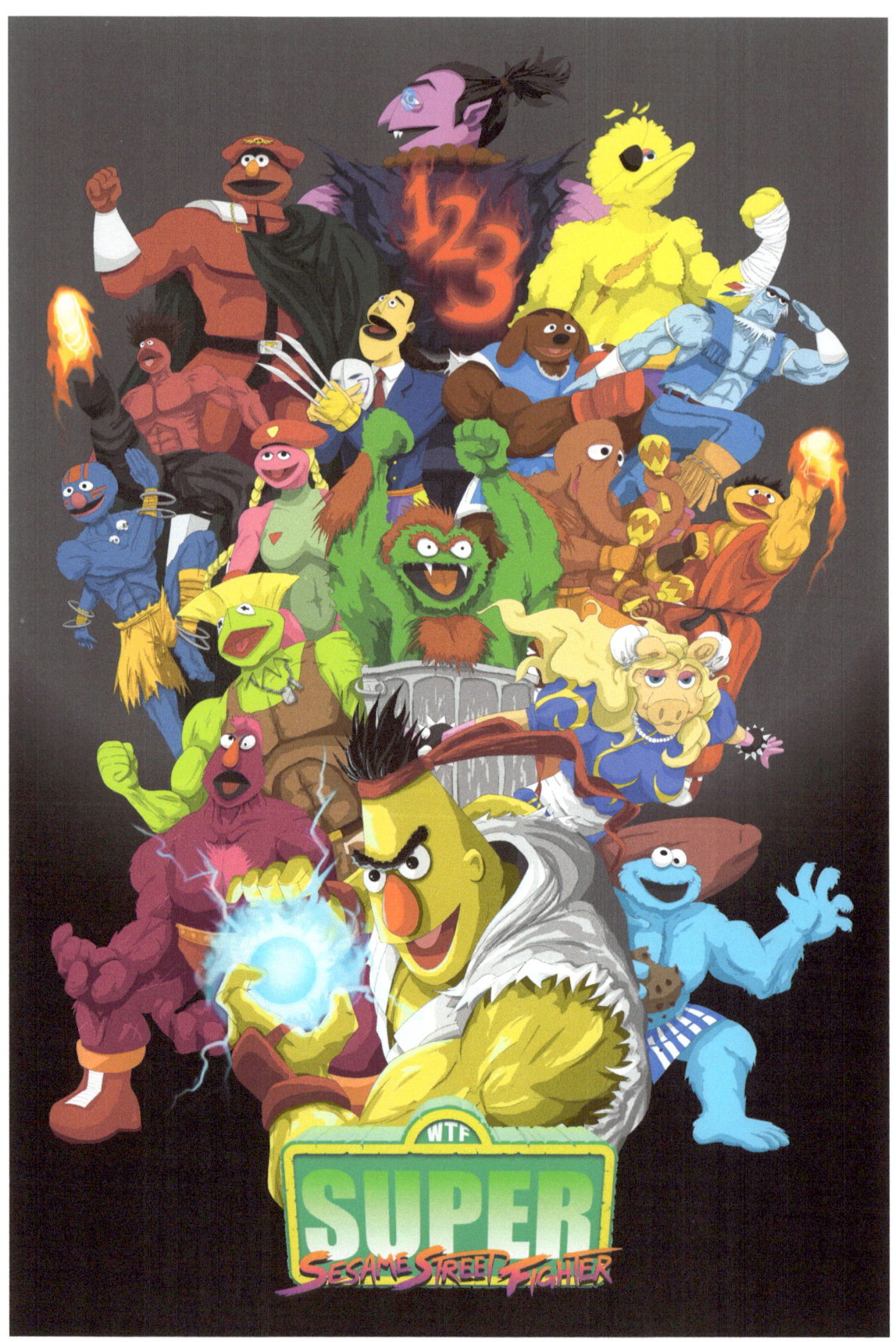

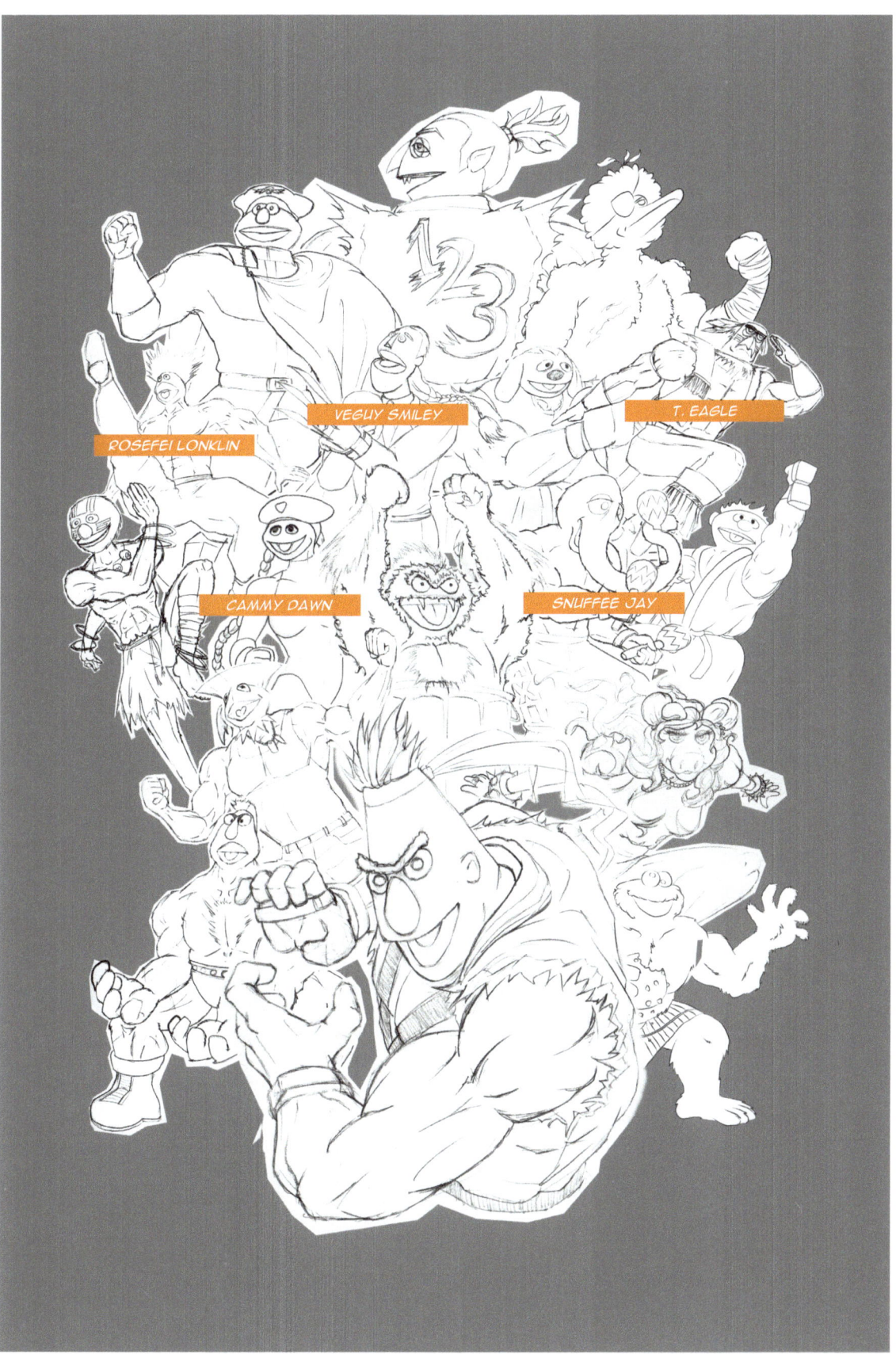

ROSEFEI LONKLIN

VEGUY SMILEY

T. EAGLE

CAMMY DAWN

SNUFFEE JAY

PENCILS/SKETCHES

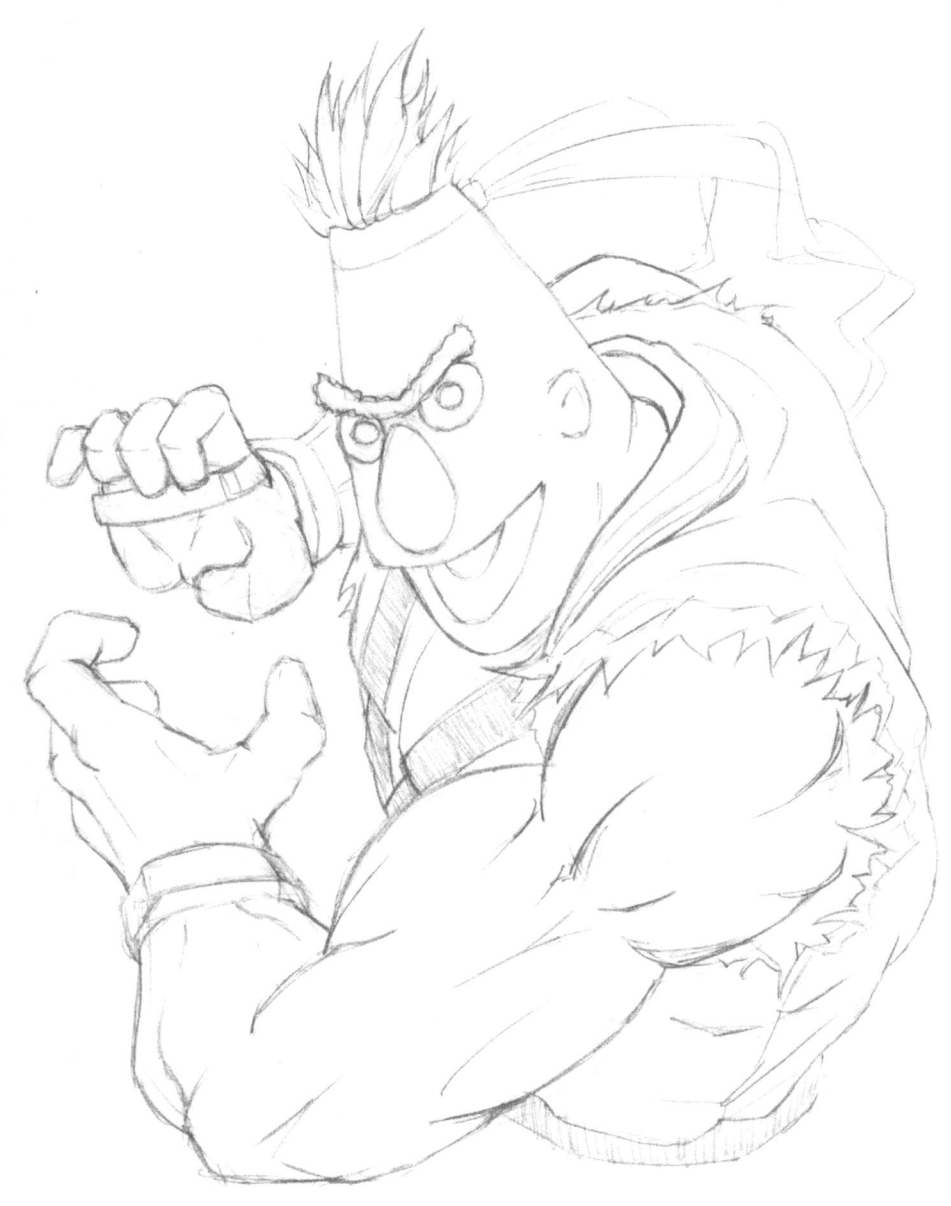

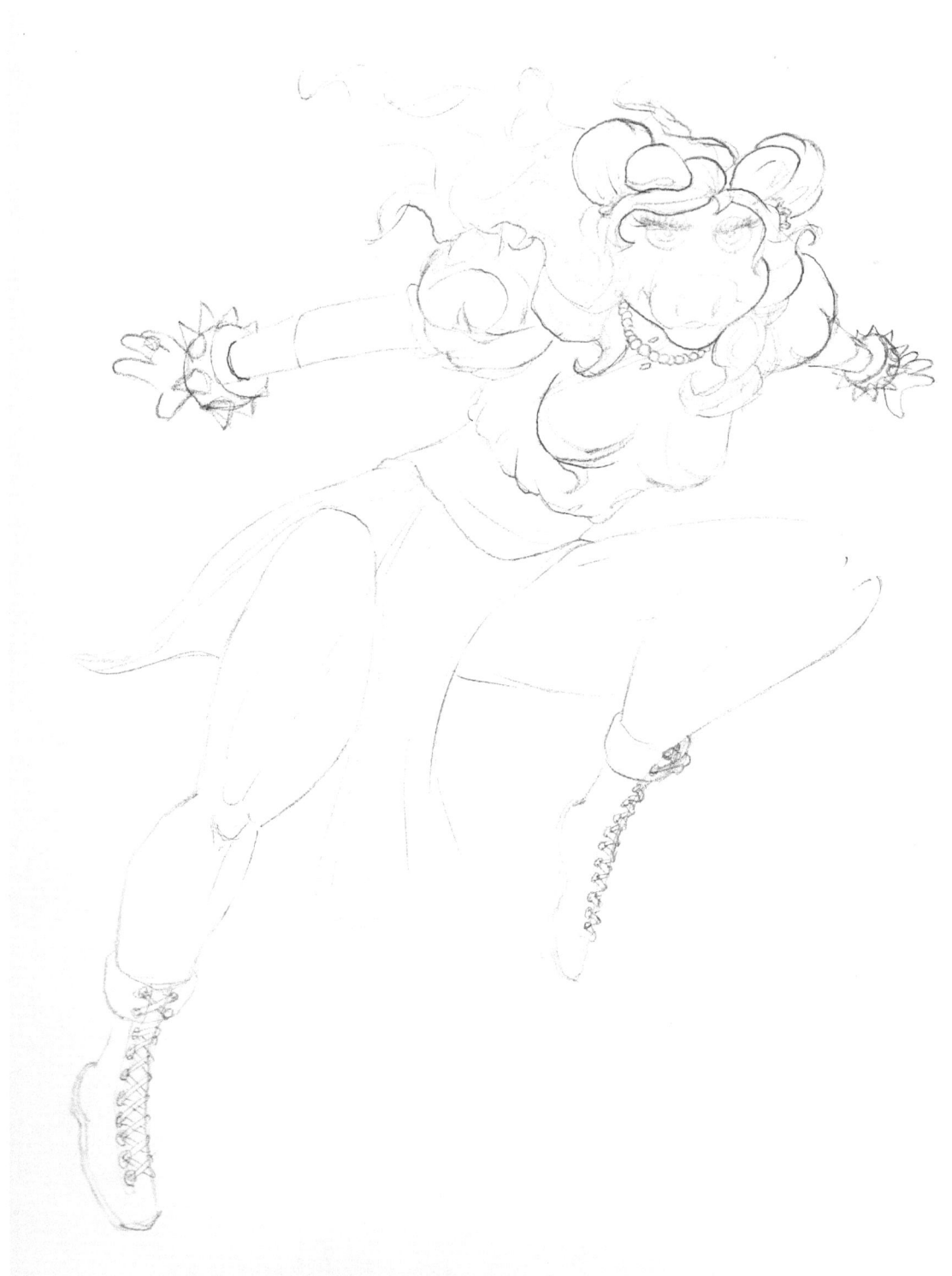

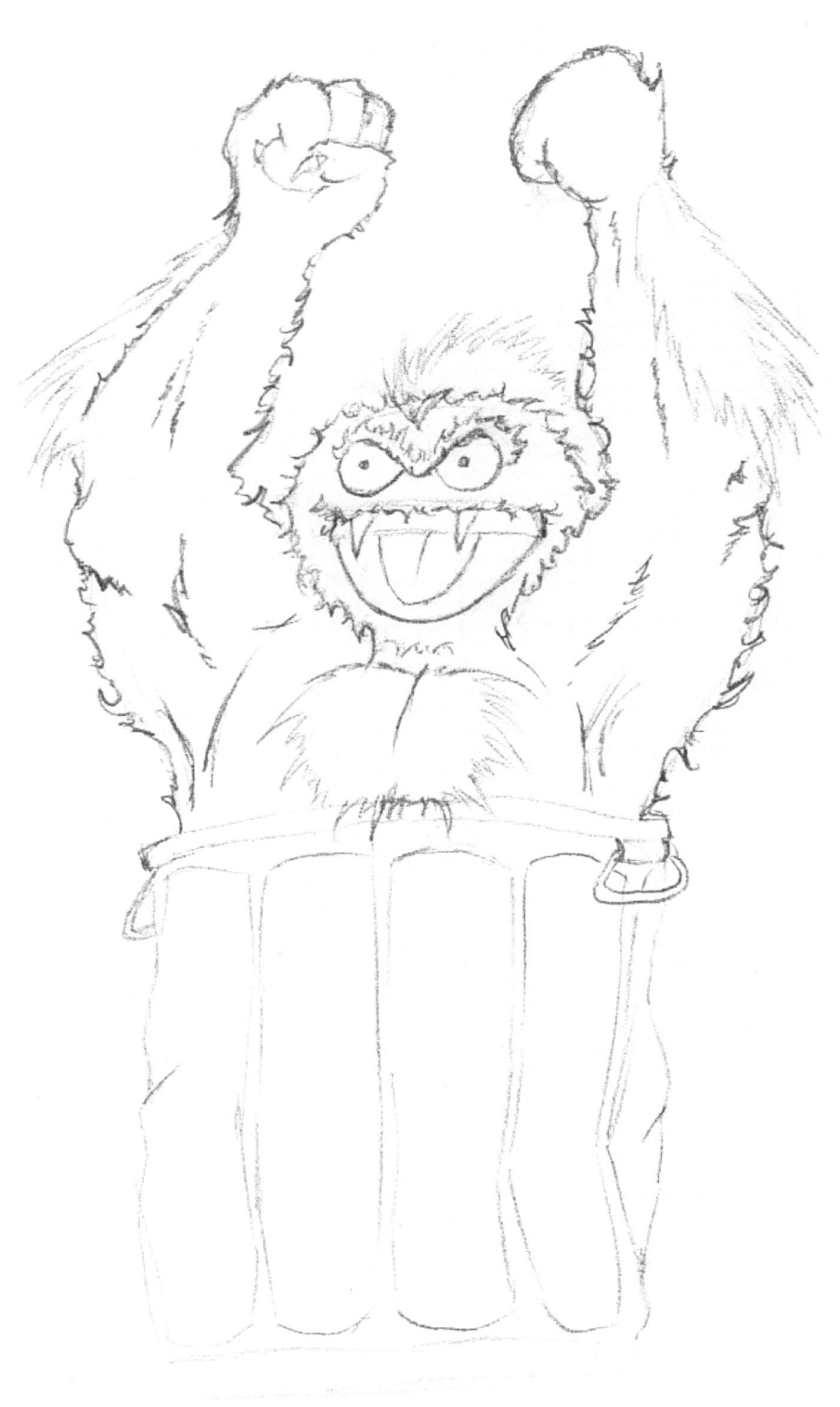

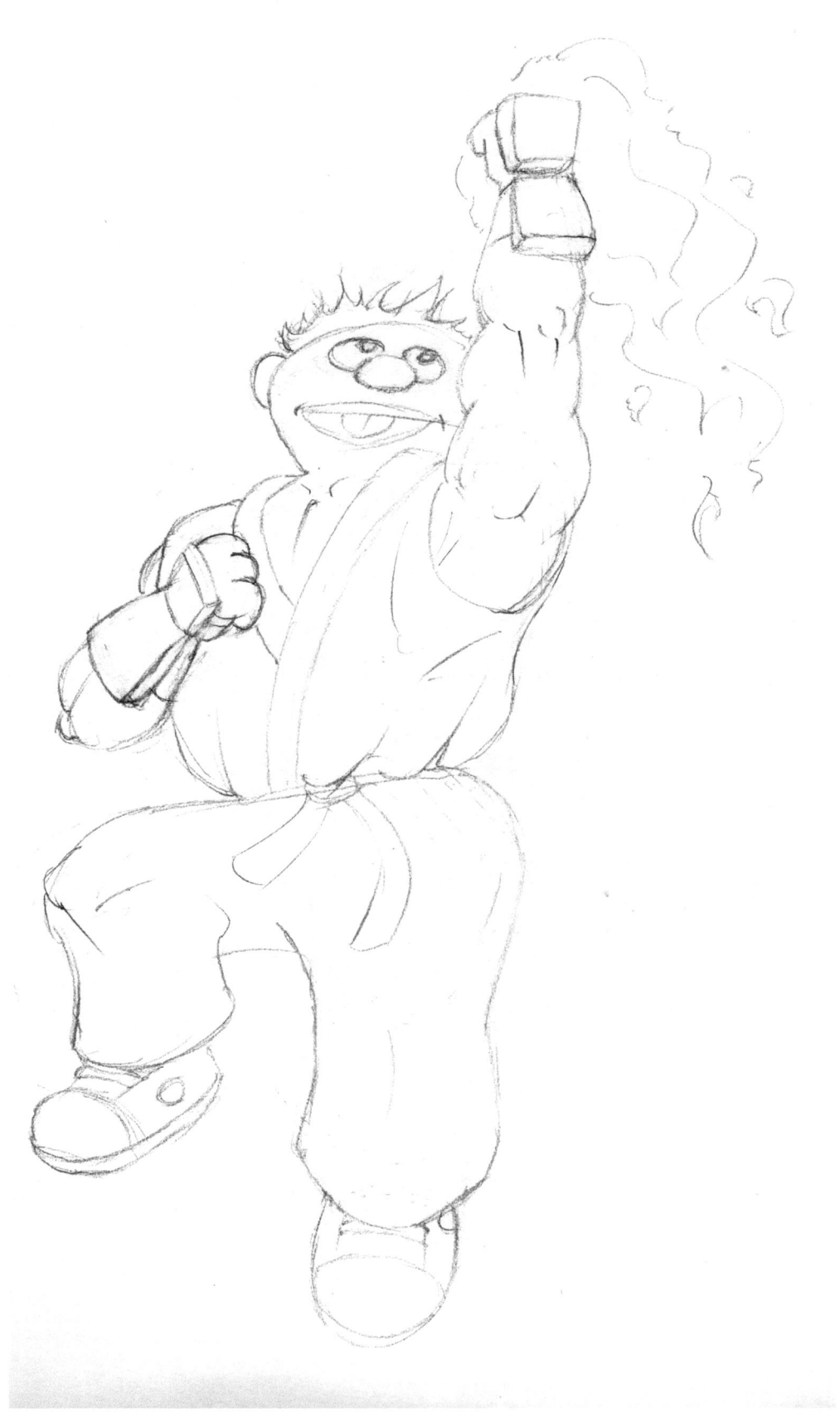

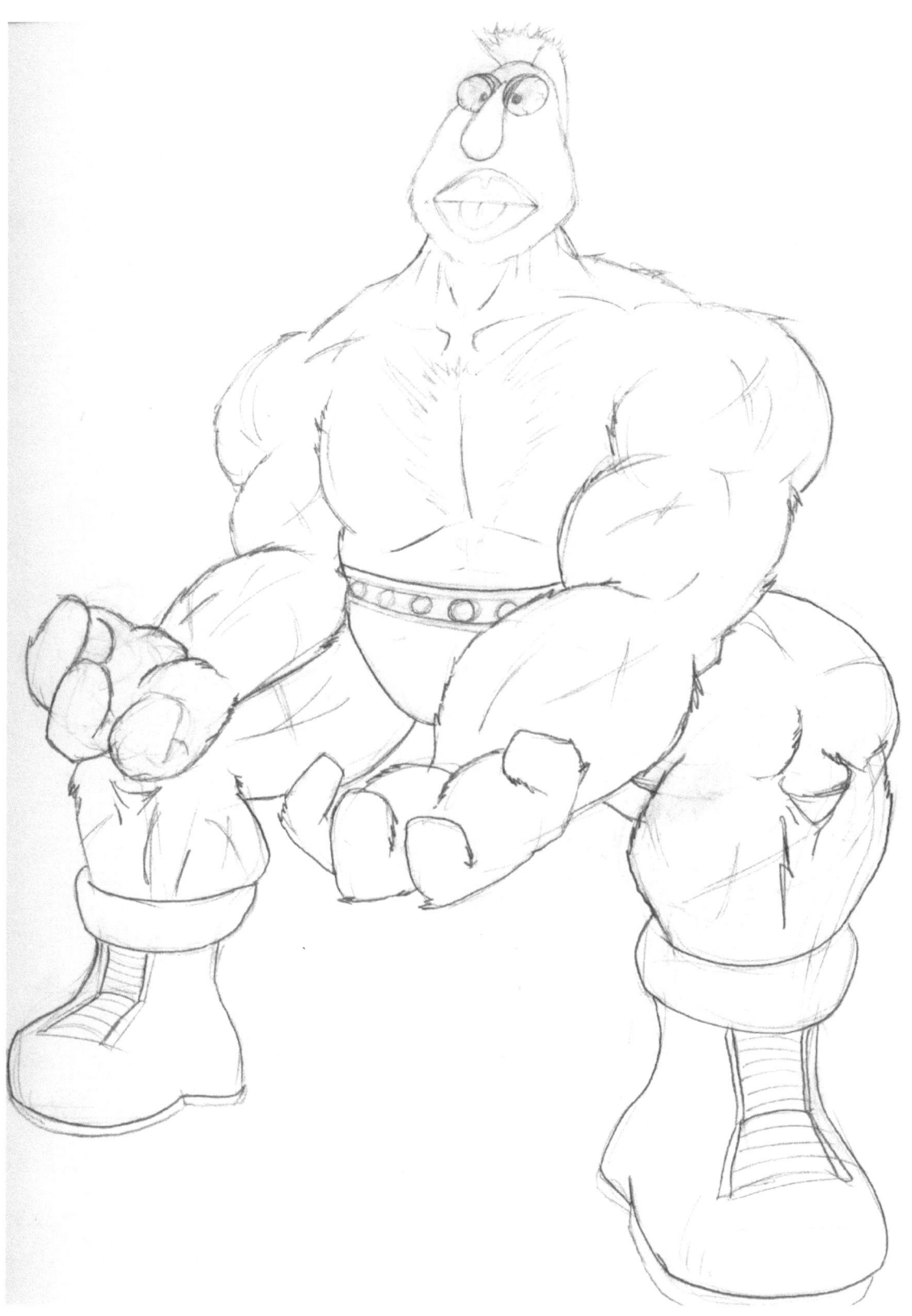

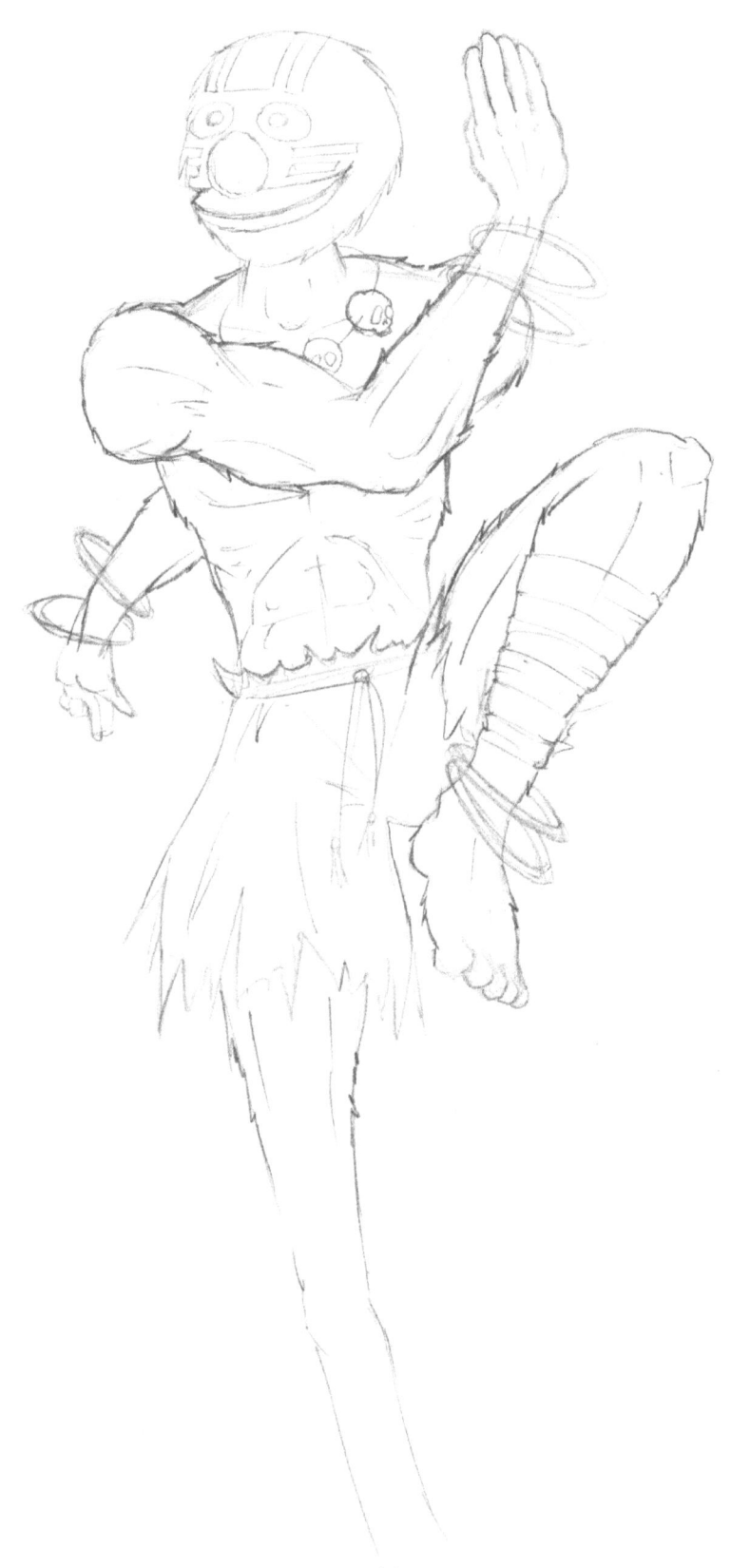

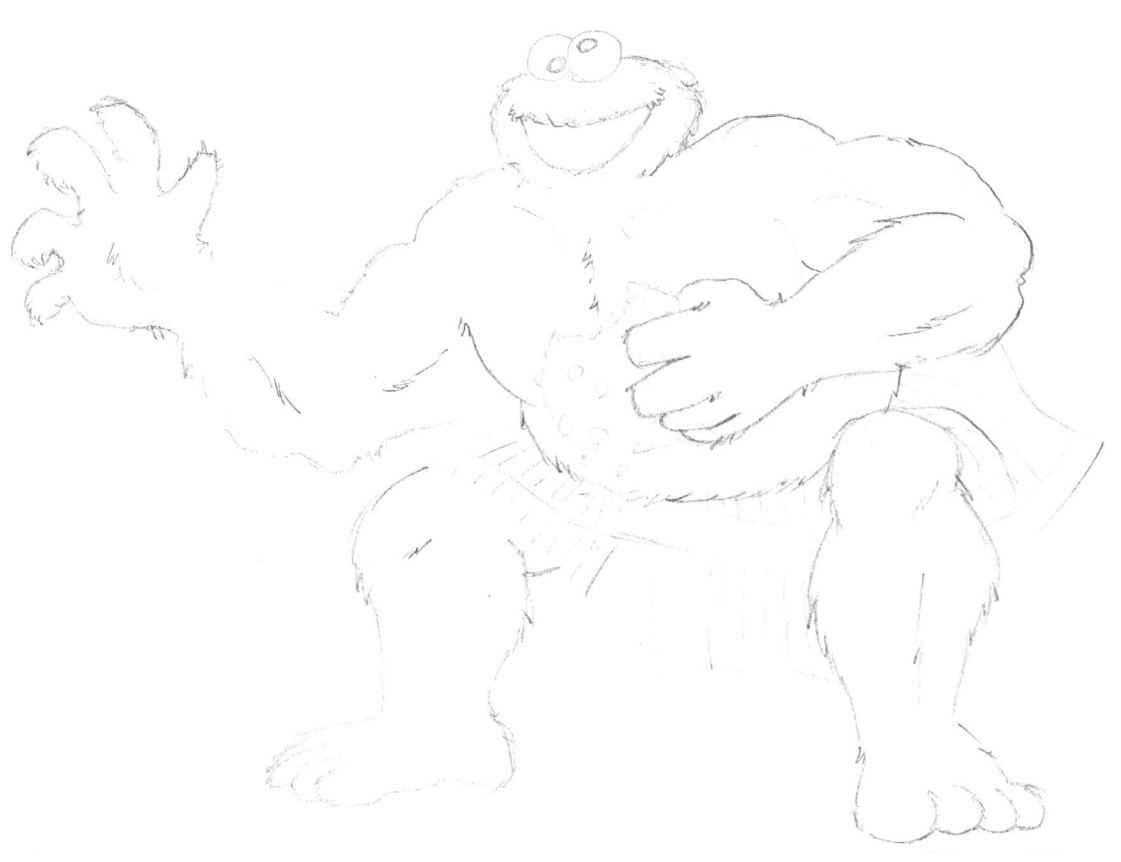

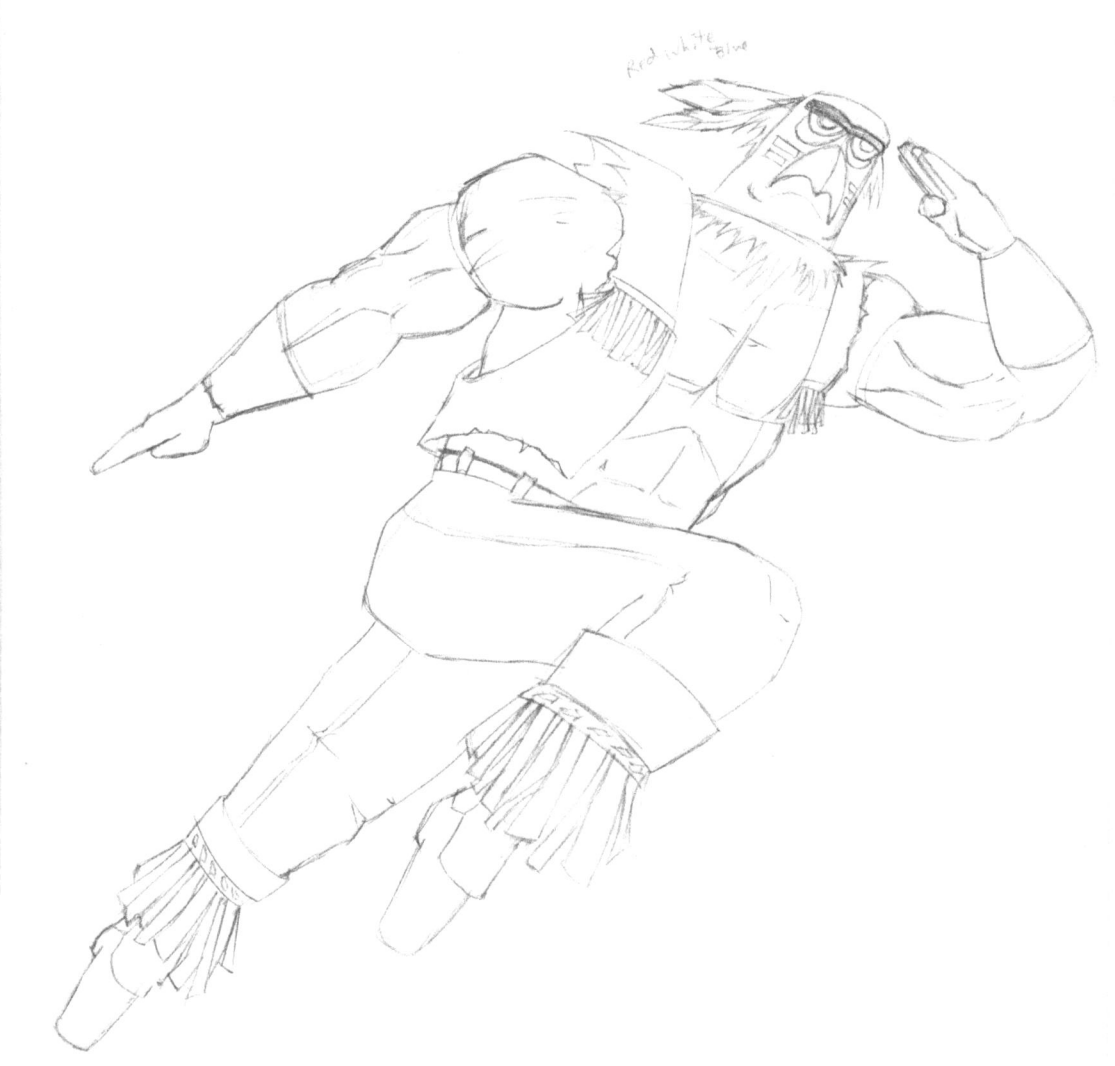

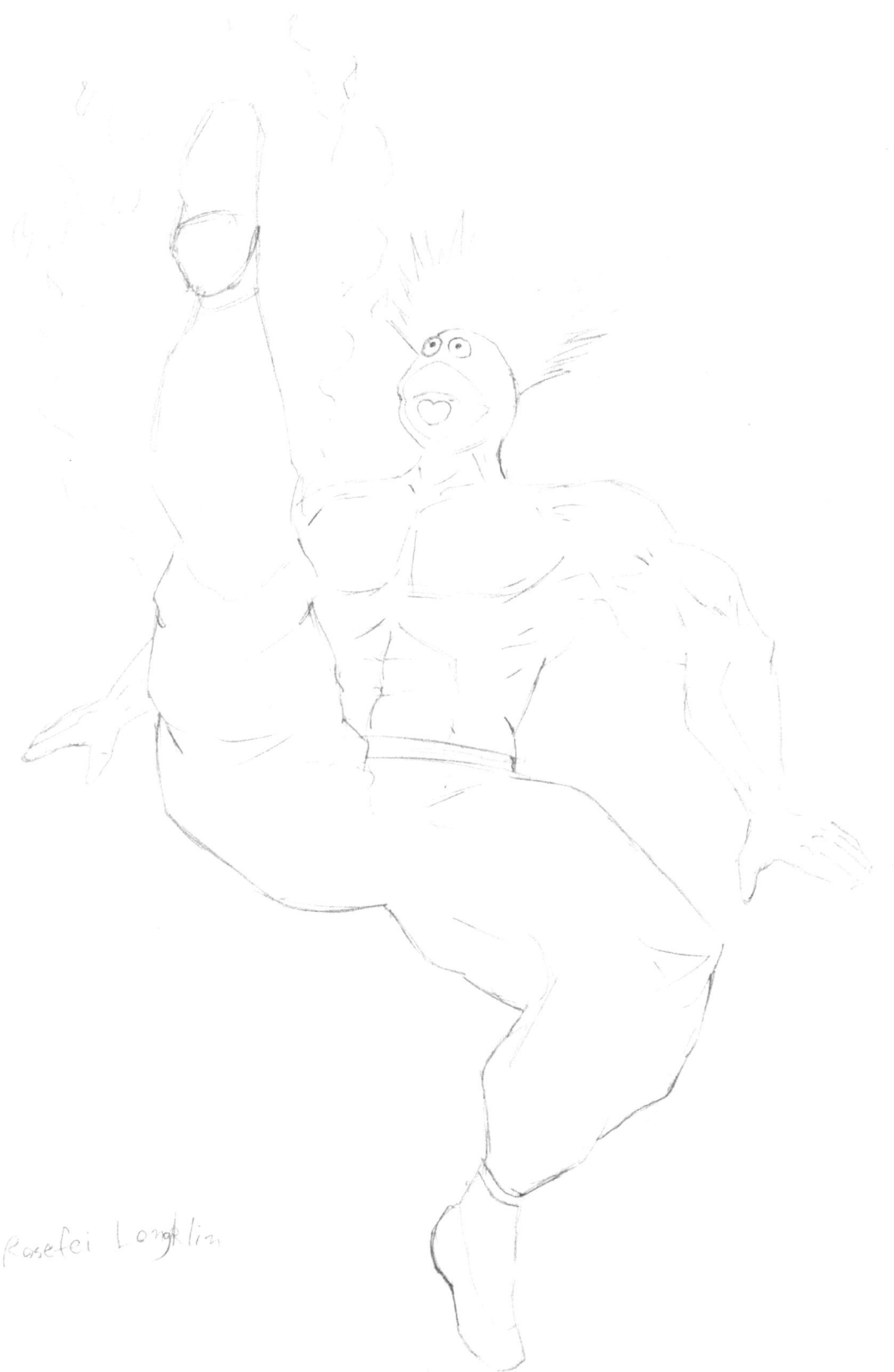

Rosefei Longlin

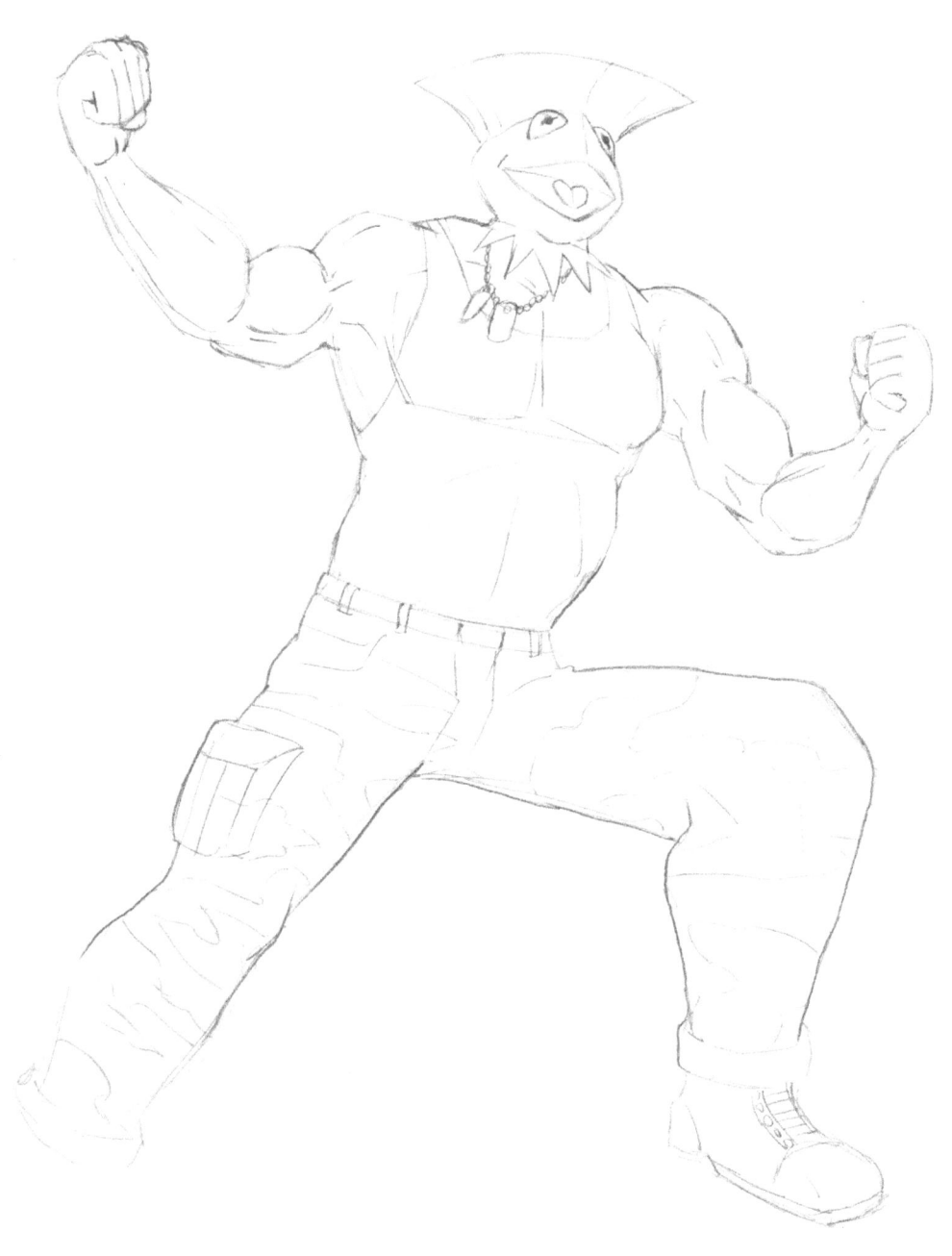

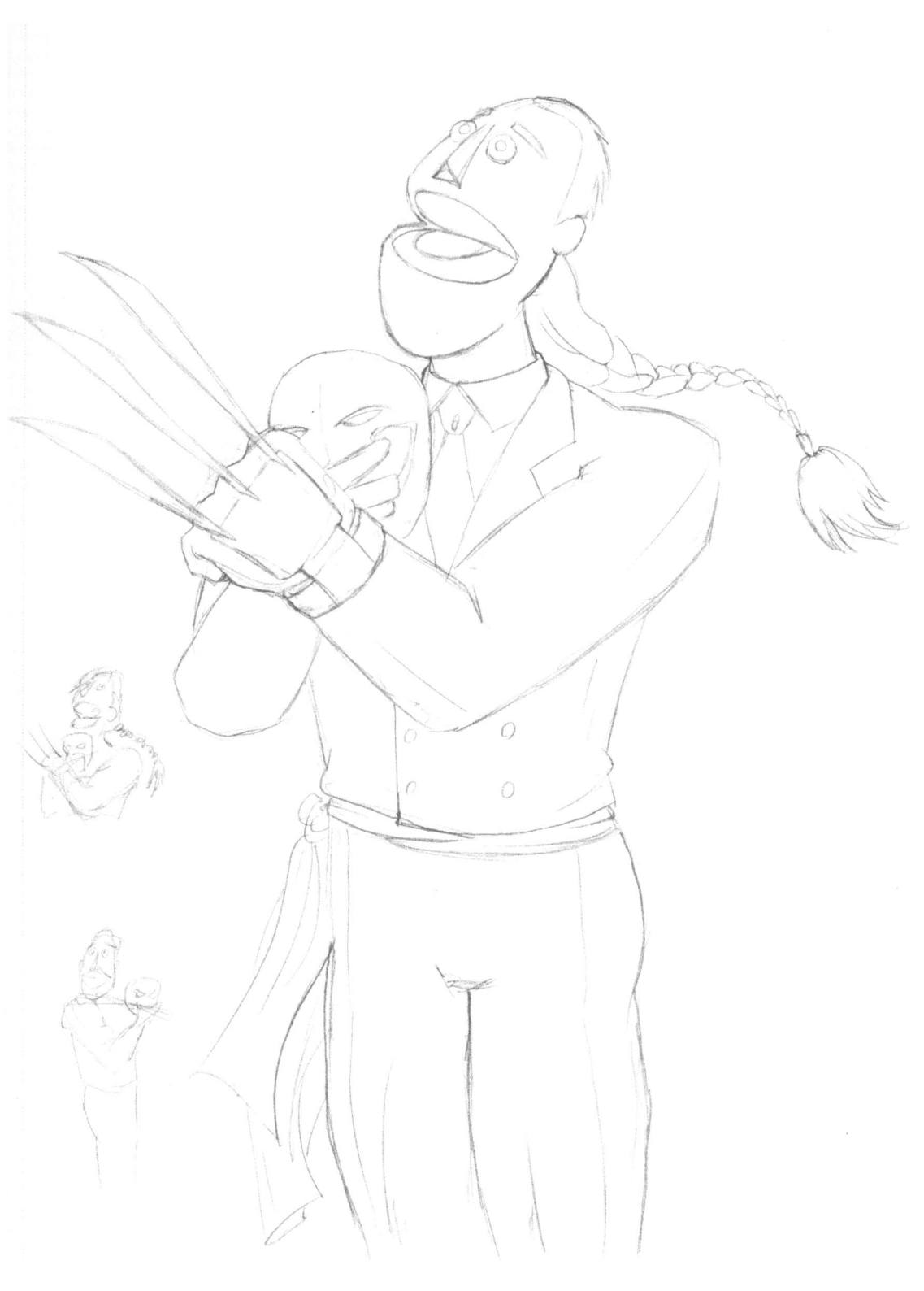

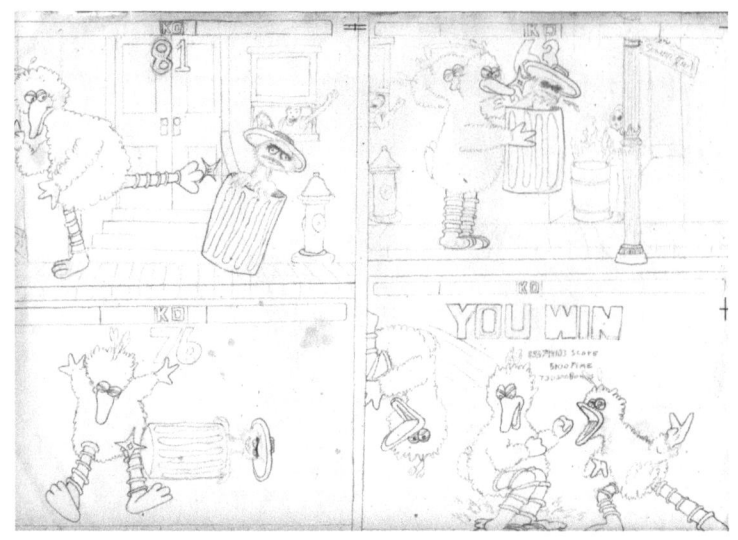

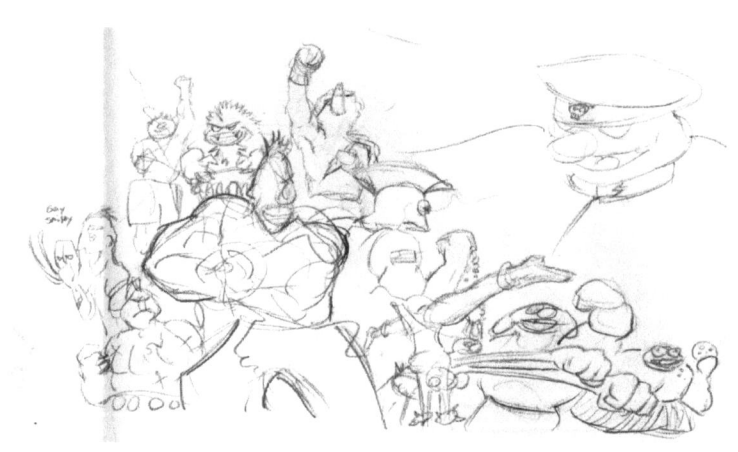

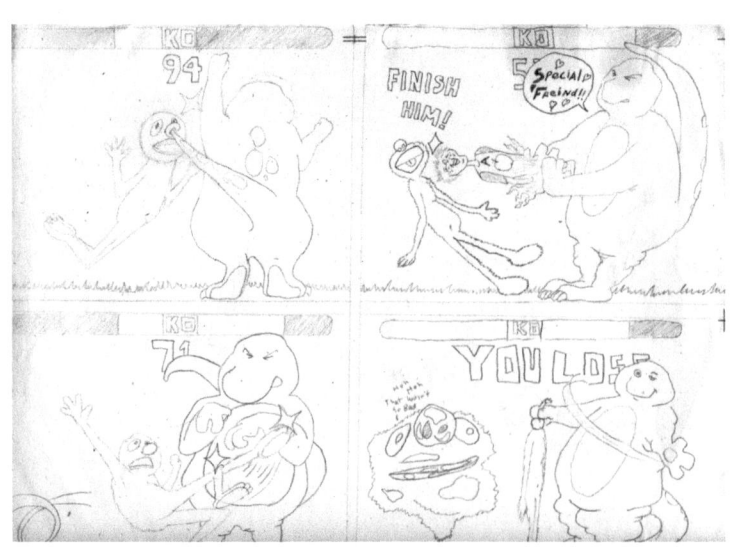

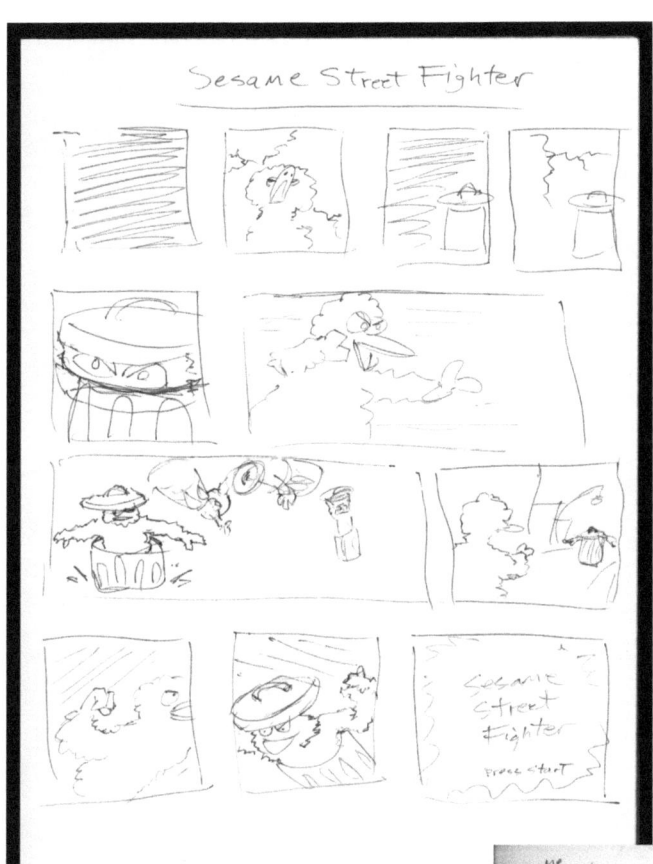

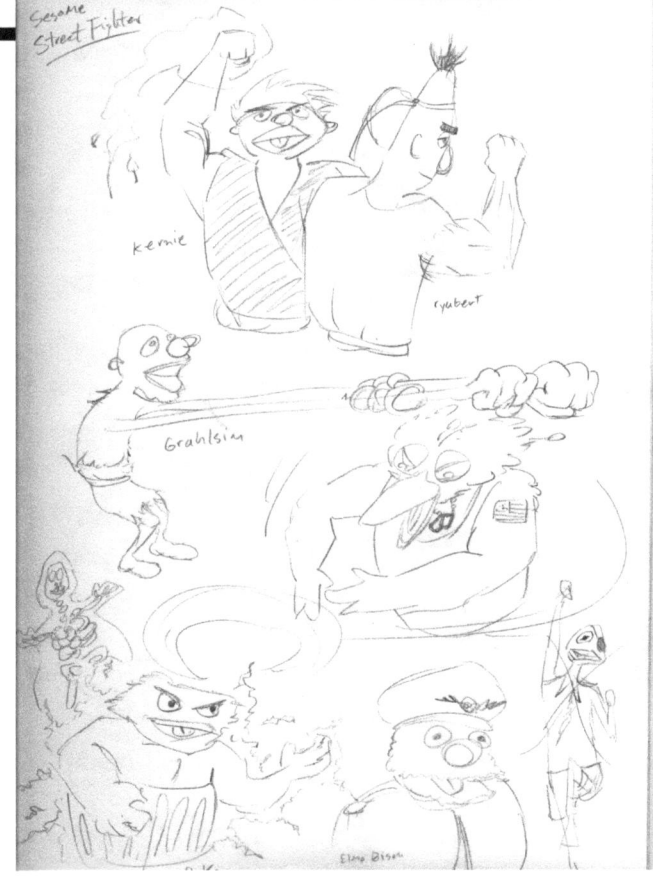

VISIT REDBUBBLE.COM
TO BUY SESAME STREET FIGHTER CLOTHING, STICKERS, IPHONE CASES AND MORE!

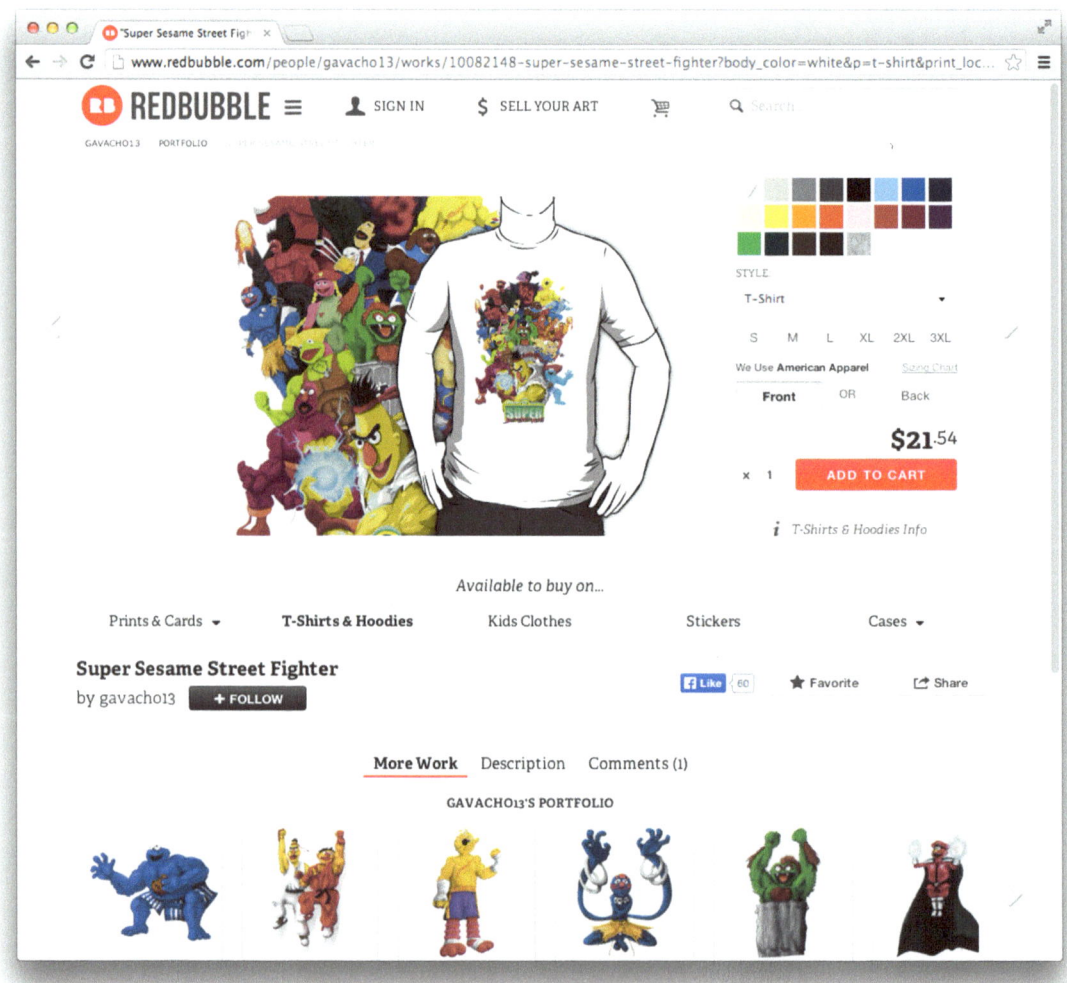

www.ingramcontent.com/pod-product-compliance
Lightning Source LLC
Chambersburg PA
CBHW050359180526
45159CB00005B/2075